Wesley
ON
SALVATION

Wesley
=ON=
SALVATION

A Study in the
Standard Sermons

Kenneth J. Collins

Foreword by Thomas C. Oden

FRANCIS ASBURY PRESS
of Zondervan Publishing House
Grand Rapids. Michigan

WESLEY ON SALVATION
Copyright © 1989 by Kenneth J. Collins

Francis Asbury Press is an imprint of Zondervan Publishing House,
1415 Lake Drive, S.E., Grand Rapids, Michigan 49506.

Library of Congress Cataloging in Publication Data

Collins, Kenneth J.
    Wesley on salvation : a study in the standard sermons / Kenneth J. Collins.
        p.   cm.
    Bibliography: p.
    ISBN 0-310-75421-6
    1. Salvation—History of doctrines—18th century. 2. Wesley, John, 1703-
1791. Sermons on several occasions. 3. Methodist Church—Doctrines—History—18th century. I. Title.
BT751.2.C64   1989
234'.092'4—dc19   89-87
                                                                     CIP

All Scripture quotations, unless otherwise noted, are taken from the HOLY
BIBLE: NEW INTERNATIONAL VERSION (North American Edition).
Copyright © 1973, 1978, 1984, by the International Bible Society. Used by
permission of Zondervan Bible Publishers.

Edited by Robert D. Wood

Printed in the United States of America

89 90 91 92 93 94 / CH / 10 9 8 7 6 5 4 3 2 1

to the Memory
of
Frank Bateman Stanger

ACKNOWLEDGMENTS

I want to express my appreciation to Dr. Melvin Dieter of Asbury Theological Seminary who read the manuscript in its early stages and who provided much useful criticism. I would also like to thank Dr. Thomas Oden, who, in his course taught at The Theological School Drew University, placed Wesley at the center of Methodist theology—where the Oxford don belongs—and for providing insights into the areas of both Wesley and Methodist studies that are nothing less than prodigious.

Kenneth J. Collins
1989

CONTENTS

FOREWORD

I commend this book to lay readers who seek a clear explication of key themes of Wesley's teaching on salvation; to pastors who may be preaching on grace, faith, and good works; and to scholars seeking rightly to place Wesley in the development of Protestant teaching.

We have every reason these days to expect an exciting, new round of serious inquiry into Wesley's Standard Sermons. Their status as doctrinal standards among Wesleyan-related churches is being gradually rediscovered and reaffirmed after some period of neglect. And interest in Wesley among other evangelicals remains high.

Kenneth Collins has made a fine contribution to this expanding discussion, both of a *practical* nature in helping us to understand the theological structure and content of the sermons, and *critically,* to help us to see where the remaining problems lie in the interpretation of the sermons and where viewpoints on them differ.

Wesley on Salvation: A Study in the Standard Sermons reaches for the very heart and center of the Wesleyan theological effort—the doctrine of salvation. The themes move soundly and sequentially from prevenient grace, through convincing grace to justification, the new birth, assurance, ethics, and Christian perfection. The interpretation comes out of a deep and sensitive immersion in primary sources, and a relentlessly critical reading of secondary sources on Wesley. This is a reliable guide to the theology of the sermons.

One point raised by Collins requires some further scholarly and probably judicial determination—the right number of those sermons rightly designated as "Standard Sermons," or "doctrinal standards." My own view of the number of sermons is that there is general agreement that at least forty-four are indisputably doctrinal standards. British Methodists are more likely to say forty-four, while Americans (following the tradition of Burwash and Harrison) are more likely to say fifty-two, or (following Sugden) fifty-three. These sermons (minimally forty-four) have been generally referred to since the mid-nineteenth century as Wesley's "Standard Sermons." A further determination is needed to define the status of the nine sermons added in the first four volumes of the thirty-two volume 1771 edition of Wesley's Collected Works. Collins states his reasons why the entire series of fifty-three should be included.

My own principal mentor, Albert C. Outler, will surely welcome a discussion of whether the Aldersgate experience was central or not to Wesley's biography. Collins argues vigorously and tenaciously that it does, against a host of critics who have in the last decade found new reasons to discount Aldersgate.

In pungent style, Collins has shown how Wesley's doctrine of prevenient grace helped him solve certain prevailing tensions in the classical Reformation treatment of the relation of total depravity, salvation by grace, human responsibility, and the offering of salvation to all. He carefully distinguishes between works prior to justifying faith and justifying faith, and between repentance and faith. He astutely elucidates similarities and differences between Luther and Wesley and Calvin and Wesley. With a special interest in ethics, Collins shows how Wesley steered a wise course among the shoals of quietism, formalism, legalism, and antinomianism. Readers looking for a concise statement of Wesley's doctrine of perfection, especially as it relates to the problem of subsequent repentance, will find it in the last chapter.

Collins has, in my view, solved the intriguing puzzle of why certain doctrines such as repentance and faith receive parallel treatments in different phases of the soteriological sequence. I suspect that the diagram on the next to last page of the book will keep Wesley scholars busy for a long time puzzling and debating over its viability. In my view, the issue is surgically defined by Collins.

Thomas C. Oden
The Theological School
Drew University
Madison, New Jersey

INTRODUCTION

Why this Book?

In the early 1980s when I was a teaching fellow at Drew University, I assisted Dr. Thomas C. Oden in his course on United Methodist Doctrine. This particular course was structured in such a way that students had the option of studying Wesley's writings in some depth as a part of their requirements, and I was given responsibility in terms of lectures and recitations for those students in the Wesley Studies track.

Toward the end of the course, I began to realize that some students could have made greater progress if they had understood Wesley's Standard Sermons more clearly. For, although it is a commonplace in Wesley Studies that the father of Methodism spoke "plain truth for plain people," his sermons were not so plain to my students. Indeed, they were often discouraged by the eighteenth-century style of the writings, the lack of suitable illustrations, and by their own inability to grasp the interrelationships of the various pieces. At this point I realized that something along the lines of a guide to the Fifty-three Standard Sermons was needed which would serve as an introduction to the primary material and which would encourage students to read Wesley for themselves. In addition, this guide, if successful, would also serve those who have already read these sermons by offering them the larger structure of the material. Both aspects, then, of content and structure would have to be addressed, and these concerns led to the production of this present work, *Wesley on Salvation: A Study in the Standard Sermons*.

Concerning the first aspect of content, if I may use an analogy drawn from biblical studies, *Wesley on Salvation* is closer in approach to literary criticism than to historical criticism. Its focus is on the text itself rather than on the

11

documentation, sources, and readings which undergird Wesley's published sermons—an area that has already been amply treated by Professors Outler, Heitzenrater, and others. In other words, what Wesley *said,* the theological world evidenced in the text, becomes more important than what he read; the *content* not the context of his thought is underscored here, though the latter does—and should—become important at times. In short, *Wesley on Salvation* is an instance of historical theology with emphasis on theology rather than on history.

Moreover, the method proposed here is not exclusive of but complementary to those approaches which seek to relate Wesley's sermon corpus to the past; that is, to the social-historical milieu from which it arose, or to the present, to the modern world and its problems. However, each transition, whether to the world of the eighteenth century or to the twentieth, should have as its point of orientation the received text. Indeed, the danger of the first transition, on the one hand, is that Wesley can very easily become "lost in the sources"—or worse yet—one may conclude that only professional theologians and historians are able to discern the "real" Wesley. The irony of all this, especially in light of Wesley's avowed intention to speak plain truth to plain people as noted earlier, deserves more than a little consideration. The danger of the second transition, on the other hand, is that the contemporary setting will be so emphasized that Wesley merely becomes a mouthpiece for modern views. Both errors, then, need to be corrected by the text itself.

Second, concerning the issue of structure, the trajectory of this present work is ostensibly the Wesleyan *ordo salutis* as displayed in the key sermon, *The Scripture Way of Salvation,* produced in 1765. To be sure, this is only one approach; others could have been taken. Moreover, the author is well aware of "the whole Wesley" and the subtle shifts in his theology that are evident especially after 1770. Nevertheless, the theological picture of the Standard Sermons develops most readily against the photographic plate of this mid-career sermon, even if that picture has to be brought into sharper focus by other considerations—and by other sermons. In other words, the present approach is heuristic, not definitive, creative, not scholastic, more suited to the practical process of discerning and applying religious *meaning* than to pedantic and airy speculation.

Not only is Wesley's order of salvation the framework for

this study, but, unlike previous works, the internal structure within his theological framework also receives significant attention. For example, many of Wesley's doctrines such as repentance, faith, and assurance receive parallel, though slightly different, treatments in other areas of the *ordo salutis*. Earlier works did little with this structure; it was simply there as a kind of chronological or sequential ordering for them. *Wesley on Salvation,* however, should rectify this.

Why Fifty-Three Sermons?

Currently, a debate continues in the United Methodist Church between Professors Oden and Heitzenrater as to whether the Constitutional Conference of the Methodist Episcopal Church in 1808 established Wesley's published sermons and his *Explanatory Notes Upon the New Testament* as standards of doctrine protected by the First Restrictive Rule. In support of his case, Dr. Heitzenrater makes a distinction between "matters that bear the force of law and those that rely on the weight of tradition,"[1] and argues that only the Articles of Religion received the first kind of legitimation. In this view, Wesley's Standard Sermons and *Notes* were not implied by the First Restrictive Rule. Dr. Oden, on the other hand, maintains that "John Wesley's *Sermons* and *Notes* have had an uninterrupted consensual history of being received as established standards of doctrine in the United Methodist Church and its predecessors."[2]

Perhaps this current debate by now is all but moot, especially since the 1988 General Conference of the United Methodist Church reaffirmed an earlier decision (See the 1972 *Discipline*) that the Standard Sermons and *Notes* constitute part of its doctrinal standards. But what remains important for discussion is the number of sermons included in this recent decision. Basically, two options are here. On the one hand, since the 1988 General Conference did not specify any particular number of sermons, its use of the phrase "Sermons and Notes" would have to refer to the entire corpus—in other words to 151 sermons. However, if all of Wesley's sermons are deemed "standard," then it appears that this term has been virtually emptied of all meaning.

On the other hand, the General Conference may have had the Constitutional Conference of 1808 in mind as it asserted its doctrinal standards in an attempt to maintain historical and traditional continuity. If this is the case, then one must ask how many sermons were protected by the First Restrictive Rule of the 1808 Conference. In other words, if one accepts Oden's claim that the First Restrictive Rule has a double reference, that is, to the Articles *and* to the sermons and *Notes,*[3] then just how many of Wesley's sermons were in view? Was it 151, 108, 53, 52, or 44? To answer this question, a little historical background is necessary.

One of the first steps that John Wesley took to render some of his sermons "standard" was the creation of a Model Deed in 1749 which restricted the use of Methodist preaching houses to those who preached according to the doctrine contained in his *Notes* and four volumes of sermons. But to which sermons did the deed refer? By the time the Model Deed was published in 1763, the four volumes contained forty-four items, forty-three sermons plus the addition of *Wandering Thoughts* in 1762, and so the reference is fairly clear. However, in the 1771 edition of his four volumes of sermons, Wesley added nine other sermons, bringing the total to fifty-three. Not content with this, he once again made a change in the 1787 edition and reverted to the forty-four. This means, of course, that the idea of fifty-three or fifty-two standard sermons (if the one on the death of George Whitefield is excluded) had a short life in British Methodism. Indeed, when the British Conference decided the matter in 1914, they considered the 1787 edition definitive.

Interestingly enough, the preceding poses a problem for the interpretation of the American situation and the current debate.[4] For if Oden's claim that the American preachers "publicly avowed their continuing indebtedness and loyalty to Wesley and their rigorous determination to maintain doctrinal union between Methodists of Europe and America"[5] is correct, then they too would have assented to forty-four sermons and not fifty-two as Oden maintains.[6] That is, the American Conference of 1808 would have been familiar with Wesley's later edition of his sermons in 1787, and therefore probably would have had forty-four sermons in mind as they affirmed the First Restrictive Rule. But who can say for sure, for the 1808 Conference neither specifically referred to the sermons and *Notes* as its doctrinal standards—although Francis Ward tried to get the Conference to go on record in this matter—nor did it fix the number of Standard Sermons. However, *if* the Constitutional Conference was, in fact, guided in its deliberations and judgments by the British publishing history of Wesley's sermons, then the situation would look something like this:

1763	The Model Deed	Forty-four Sermons
1771	Edition of the Works	Fifty-three Sermons
1787	Edition of the Sermons	Forty-four Sermons
1808	American Conference	Forty-four Sermons

So, then, if the 1988 General Conference of the United Methodist Church has specified that Wesley's sermons constitute part of its doctrinal standards, is it reasonable to infer that the reference is only to forty-four sermons?

The outcome of these discussions within the United Methodist Church remains to be seen; related issues, no doubt, need to be addressed and clarified. But there are still at least two good reasons why any study on Wesley's Standard Sermons should take fifty-three items as its focus and not forty-four, despite some of the evidence just cited.

First of all, Albert Outler reasons that since Wesley, at the heyday of his career (age 68), preferred the order in the 1771 edition, then fifty-three sermons should be of special concern.[7] He also cautions that the omission of the additional sermons beyond the forty-four "would represent a serious loss"[8] in terms of any overview of Wesley's theology. Without a doubt, the sermons *On Sin in Believers, The Repentance of Believers,* and *The Scripture Way of Salvation* are vital if one wants to understand the essential order which the sermons evidence.

Second, the Burwash edition of the Standard Sermons, which contains fifty-two pieces (the sermon on George Whitefield is omitted), has gone through numerous printings and has had a long history in both the United States and Canada and is still in print. Likewise, Sugden's edition of Wesley's Fifty-Three Standard Sermons has recently been reprinted by Abingdon and Francis Asbury Press for American consumption. So if one asks what, in fact, American college and seminary students and laypeople are reading, the answer is some form of the Fifty-Three Sermons, and so we must proceed accordingly. Therefore, when this study uses the terms "Standard Sermons" or "Fifty-Three Standard Sermons" it is not adjudicating the numerical problem but is simply referring to the popular title of a body of literature. In other words, the terms are used and retained for their descriptive, not necessarily their prescriptive, value.

What is the Value of Reading the Fifty-Three Standard Sermons?

In his Preface to the Standard Sermons, Wesley reveals not only his concern to write *ad populum,* that is, for the masses, but also his basic purpose in producing these homilies which is none other than to teach "the essentials of true religion."[9] The one thing desirable to know, he writes, "is the way to heaven, how to land safe on that happy shore."[10] Indeed, in a certain sense, his sermons are a map or guide to the Scriptures showing the way of God concerning salvation as opposed to the inventions of people. The sermons, then, do not treat matters of a highly speculative nature such as the process of creation or proofs for the existence of God. Instead, they are instances of practical theology, concerned with the day-to-day problems of entering into and living the Christian life. Wesley employs the image of an arrow in flight to convey his design:

> I have thought, I am a creature of a day, passing through life as an arrow through the air. I am a spirit come from God, and returning to God . . . I want to know one thing—the way to heaven; how to land safe on that happy shore. God Himself has condescended to teach the way; for this very end He came from heaven. He hath written it down in a book. O give me that book! At any price, give me the book of God! I have it: here is knowledge enough for me.[11]

In addition, Wesley's sermons appear to be especially relevant today because they treat in a significant way the leading problem of this age: how can a personal faith in Jesus Christ go beyond self-concern to minister to the neighbor and to society as a whole? Put another way, how can the circle of redemption be drawn ever larger? All those, then, who desire to live out the truths of theology instead of being content with a discussion of them, all those who are eager to move from theory to practice by applying the truths of the Bible not only to personal life but also to social life, would do well to study Wesley's Fifty-Three Standard Sermons.

NOTES

[1] Richard P. Heitzenrater, "At Full Liberty: Doctrinal Standards in Early American Methodism," *Quarterly Review* Vol. 5, No. 3 (Fall 1985), 8.

[2] Thomas C. Oden, "Methodist Doctrinal Standards: Reply to Richard Heitzenrater," *Quarterly Review* Vol. 7, No. 1 (Spring 1987), 41–42. See also Dr. Oden's book which contains a thorough analysis of the entire issue: *Doctrinal Standards in the Wesleyan Tradition* (Grand Rapids: Zondervan/Francis Asbury Press, 1988).

[3] *Doctrinal Standards in the Wesleyan Tradition*, p. 42.

[4] Edward H. Sugden, ed., *Wesley's Standard Sermons*, 2 vols. (London: The Epworth Press, 1921), I, 14. Also see his discussion in volume 2, pp. 331ff., concerning the Conference and the Fifty-Three Sermons.

[5] Thomas C. Oden, *Doctrinal Standards in the Wesleyan Tradition*, p. 40.

[6] Ibid., p. 23. Here Oden follows Burwash's numbering. Cf. Nathaniel Burwash, *Wesley's Doctrinal Standards* (Salem, Ohio: Convention Book Store, 1967), pp. x–xviii.

[7] Albert C. Outler, ed., *The Works of John Wesley*, 34 vols. (Nashville: Abingdon Press, 1984), I, 43.

[8] Ibid., p. 44.

[9] Ibid., p. 103.

[10] Ibid., p. 105.

[11] Ibid., pp. 104–05.

I

DIVINE GRACE AND HUMAN SIN:
Prevenient Grace and Original Sin

THE EVER-PRESENT GRACE OF GOD

The principal ingredient in Wesley's theology, from which all else has its origin, is the grace of God. In several places in his works, he notes that not only was grace manifested at creation, but it will also be present at the consummation of all things. In other words, grace, unlike the wrath of God, is from *beginning* to end; it precedes, sustains, and follows humanity. In fact, at no point in Wesley's theology of salvation is divine grace not the leading motif, whether one is considering the origin of humanity or any step along the way in the process of redemption. Every interpretation of his theology, therefore, that fails to take this important ingredient into account in a significant way will, undoubtedly, be wide of the mark. Simply put, in Wesley's theology, grace is the first chord struck in God's creation, and in this present work as well.

More specifically, in his Standard Sermons Wesley defines the grace of God in two key ways. Like the continental reformers before him, he views grace, first of all, as the "undeserved favor"[1] of God: "All the blessings which God hath bestowed upon man are of his mere grace, bounty, or favour: his free, undeserved favour, favour altogether undeserved. . ."[2] But, secondly, his extensive readings in the Greek Christian heritage[3] helped him to see grace in another way, as "the power of the Holy Ghost"[4] to enable people to walk in the ways of God. The former understanding accents the divine/human relation; the latter, human participation and renewal. Along these lines it has often been argued that Wesley brings together a

19

Protestant conception of grace and a "Catholic" conception of holiness. While this claim is to some extent true, it is important to observe that these two emphases can be seen *within* his conception of grace itself. For Wesley, the grace of God involves not only declaring sinners to be just but actually transforming, assisting, and renewing them as well. By this understanding, therefore, Wesley has in place at the outset some of the major planks which will undergird his subsequent thought and distinguish it from others. Moreover, though these two senses of grace are woven throughout his writings, the particular sense which is emphasized often depends on the subject under review.

When Wesley describes the state of humanity prior to the Fall, he underscores grace not in the second sense as empowerment by the Holy Spirit, but as the favor, bounty, or goodness of God. "It was free grace that 'formed man of the dust of the ground,' he writes, 'and breathed into him a living soul.' "[5] Elsewhere he affirms the initial goodness of creation in that "every creature was 'good' in its primeval state."[6] However, with the exception of the sermon *Salvation by Faith* there is actually little discussion in the Standard Sermons of the gracious condition of humanity prior to the Fall, although this subject is treated in other homilies. This fact can be best explained by an appeal to Wesley's purpose in the Standard Sermons which is immensely practical: that is, he is largely concerned with the present condition of his congregations, a condition that is not characterized by Adamic innocence but by the effects of the Fall.

ORIGINAL SIN

During the Enlightenment of the eighteenth century, several English, French, and German authors reexamined the traditional conception of human nature under the "new" watchwords of reason, nature, and progress with the result that a more optimistic view of human nature replaced an earlier pessimism. When such a shift was expressed in religious terms, it often took the form of Deism. Matthew Tindal, for example, in his book *Christianity As Old As Creation* argued that the Fall and the notion of original guilt were demeaning to humanity and that such notions belonged to the superstitious past. Likewise, in 1740, Dr. John Taylor, although not a Deist but a

Dissenting minister, published *The Scripture Doctrine of Original Sin: Proposed to Free and Candid Examination* in which original sin was deemed a fiction.

Specifically in relation to the latter work John Wesley decided to pick up his pen in opposition. In 1757, he published a lengthy treatise on the subject entitled *The Doctrine of Original Sin: According to Scripture, Reason, and Experience.* But it was not until two years later that he reduced this massive work to the more readable and popular sermon form. Thus, Wesley's sermon *Original Sin* was first of all an apologetical endeavor, composed to state clearly and succinctly one of the historic truths of Christianity that was broadly under attack in the eighteenth century.

Original Sin contains three major divisions: first, what humanity was before the flood; second, what it is now; and third, a few inferences. In the first part, Wesley notes that human hearts before the Flood were evil, contrary to moral rectitude, to the nature of God, to the divine will, and to the holy image of God wherein humanity was originally created.[7] Moreover, Wesley states emphatically that neither was any light intermixed with darkness nor was there any intermission of this evil.[8] As expressed in Genesis 6:5, the main text for this sermon, God looked down upon humanity and saw that their hearts were only evil continually.

When Wesley considers humanity in the present, he makes it clear that he is concerned with its "natural state," that is, its condition unassisted by the grace of God. In this state, humanity is blind to the things of God, and is not sensible of its spiritual needs. Before God opens their eyes, men and women are atheists in the world, having no knowledge and consequently no love of God, for they cannot love the God they do not know.[9] "We have by nature," Wesley continues, "not only no love, but no fear of God."[10] Without the grace of God, therefore, all people are rank idolaters, filled with pride, self-will, and love of the world. Their hearts are overrun with all manner of vanity: with the desire of the flesh, the desire of the eye, and the pride of life so that the present human condition is no better than that before the Flood. Wesley writes:

> The whole head is sick, and the whole heart faint. From the sole of the foot even unto the head there is no soundness, but wounds and bruises and putrifying sores. The same account is given by all the apostles, yea, by the

whole tenor of the oracles of God. From all these we learn concerning man in his natural state, unassisted by the grace of God, that "all the imaginations of the thoughts of his heart" are still "evil, only evil," and that continually.[11]

In four other sermons Wesley reiterates this same theme of utter corruption.[12] To be sure, that persons in the natural state are void of all good, wholly fallen, and totally corrupted[13] became a shibboleth for him and marked the difference between Christianity and heathenism. On this score, there is little difference between Wesley and the continental Reformers. Both Luther[14] and Calvin[15] employed negative superlatives similar to the Wesleyan phrases "wholly fallen" and "totally corrupted" to characterize humanity apart from the grace of God. But why did Wesley consider the doctrine of original sin a watershed, a fundamental doctrine? The answer lies in the connection he drew between original sin and the new birth. "Know your disease," Wesley writes, "Know your cure! Ye were born in sin; therefore ye must be born again. . . . By nature ye are wholly corrupted; by grace ye shall be wholly renewed."[16] Thus, in Wesley's mind, a weak doctrine of original sin could only result in an equally weak doctrine of the new birth. For if the extensiveness of the problem was relinquished or soft-pedaled, the radical nature of the solution would be lost as well. Little wonder, then, that the doctrine of original sin was so important to him.

Another inference that Wesley draws in his sermon *Original Sin* concerns the nature of religion. In his estimation, the religion of Jesus Christ is none other than θεραπεία ψυχῆς (therapeia psyches) "God's method of healing a soul which is *thus diseased*."[17] In other words, the task of the Savior is that of a physician who restores to its health a human soul that has been corrupted in all its powers. The great end of religion, therefore, is that of renewing human hearts in the image of God, "repairing that total loss of righteousness and true holiness which we sustained by the sin of our first parent."[18] Moreover, Wesley affirms that any religion which stops short of this is a poor farce and a mockery of God.[19]

PREVENIENT GRACE

When Wesley writes of the image of God, the *imago dei,* in his sermon *The New Birth,* he does so under three aspects. The first, the natural image, entails the idea that humans are spiritual beings endued with understanding, freedom of the will and various affections.[20] The second is the political image which points to humanity's governance of the earth. And the last aspect is the moral image which displays the "righteousness and true holiness"[21] in which humanity was originally created. According to Wesley, the effect of the Fall on the *imago dei* is such that the first two aspects were greatly marred, but the last was utterly obliterated; humanity, therefore, was now both unrighteous and unholy.

Once again, initially Wesley's conception of the Fall and its effects on humanity looks very much like Lutheran and Reformed notions. However, in a sermon written in the latter part of his career, Wesley, astonishingly, denies that a person utterly lacking the grace of God does in fact exist. In *On Working Out Our Own Salvation,* he notes:

> For allowing that all souls of men are dead in sin by nature, this excuses none, seeing there is no man that is in a state of mere nature; there is no man, unless he has quenched the Spirit, that is wholly void of the grace of God. No man living is entirely destitute of what is vulgarly called "natural conscience." But this is not natural; it is more properly termed "preventing grace." Every man has a greater or less measure of this, which waiteth not for the call of man.[22]

The idea of prevenient grace (that grace which literally "goes before" sanctifying grace) is also found in Wesley's sermon *The Scripture Way of Salvation* where he again strongly associates it with the operations of conscience. Beyond this, prevenient grace involves in some measure a re-inscription of the law of God upon human hearts so that all people have at least a general notion of right and wrong.[23] Moreover, this grace restores a measure of free will, enough to render people responsible and accountable in God's sight, and it also illumines the mind in order that the most basic attributes of God can at least be dimly perceived by reason. In other words, the doctrine of prevenient grace reveals that God takes the first step in the process of salvation and heals some of the most damaging effects of original sin. The result of this divine action is that humanity now has sufficient grace to be able to respond to God's free offer of salvation in Jesus Christ. Thus, God has not forsaken humanity in its most abject state, but has already acted through His Son Jesus Christ by that "true light that enlightens every man" (John 1:9). Wesley writes:

> Everyone has some measure of that light, some faint glimmering ray, which sooner or later, more or less, enlightens every man that cometh into the world. And everyone, unless he be one of the small number whose conscience is seared as with a hot iron, feels more or less uneasy when he acts contrary to the light of his own conscience. So that no man sins because he has not grace, but because he does not use the grace which he hath.[24]

Two further points must be noted. First, this grace as divine empowerment is rooted in the incarnation and atonement of Jesus Christ. Grace is one of the benefits of His life, work, and sacrifice; and it is, therefore, thoroughly christologically based. Second, this grace is free in all, meaning that it does not depend on any human merit or power, and it is also free for all, indicating that none are excluded from its benefits. Its reach is universal, not limited and exclusive, but inclusive.[25]

It is interesting to note, however, that if Wesley truly held a notion of total depravity—and the Standard Sermons offer no reason to doubt this—it logically follows that "irresistible grace" had to find some place in the Wesleyan order of salvation since humans in the natural state do not even have the freedom or ability to accept or reject any offered grace. Therefore, it is prevenient grace which must be irresistibly given in order to restore humanity's very ability to respond to the further grace of God. In other words, to deny that prevenient grace is irresistible is also to deny that Wesley held a doctrine of *total* depravity. One of the chief differences, then, between Calvinism and Wesleyanism is at the point in the *ordo salutis* where irresistible grace occurs. For Calvin, it is sanctifying grace which is irresistible; for Wesley, it is prevenient grace which "waiteth not for the call of man." The difference is important.

It should be pointed out, though, that Wesley employed the phrases "natural man" and "natural state" in two quite distinct senses. This has led to great confusion in Wesley studies among those scholars who have failed to appreciate the difference.[26] On the one hand, in the sermon *Original Sin,* the natural state is depicted as exclusive of the grace of God. Here Wesley wanted to consider humanity steeped in original sin, left to its own devices, and "unassisted by the grace of God."[27] But, as has already been pointed out, such a person does not exist, for there are no people without divine prevenient grace. In this first context, then, the natural state is a theoretical construct which lacks empirical verification. It is an ingredient in any full-orbed systematic theology, but it plays little role in a practical theology, for no human being is so marred and fallen.

On the other hand, the phrases "natural man" and "natural state" which appear in the sermons *Awake, Thou That Sleepest,* preached by Charles in 1742, and *The Spirit of Bondage and of Adoption* preached by John in 1746 correspond to real flesh and blood individuals, not to theoretical constructs. In the former sermon, for example, the natural state depicts a spiritual darkness in which sinners are satisfied in their sins and are content to remain in a fallen state.[28] Likewise, in the latter sermon, the state of the "natural man" is one of spiritual sleep. Here the spiritual senses are not awake; the eyes of the understanding are closed, and the law of God is virtually unknown. Furthermore, in at least three instances in *The Spirit of Bondage and of Adoption,* John Wesley associates the "natural man" with real people, and in this particular case with "the heathen."[29]

Thus it should be apparent by now the confusion which results when the disclaimer of the sermon *On Working Out Our Own Salvation* (no one is left in the natural state) is not correctly applied to the sermon *Original Sin,* as it should be, but is instead applied to the sermons *Awake, Thou That Sleepest* and *The Spirit of Bondage and Of Adoption.* When this error is made, one can only conclude that the Wesleys did not believe that there exist people in a state of spiritual darkness who are satisfied in their sins. But such a conclusion is obviously false.

By way of summary, then, although the continental Reformers and Wesley all assented to a doctrine of total depravity, the basic contours of their theologies are distinct, due to different conceptions of grace. Thus, Wesley's doctrine of prevenient grace allows him to hold together, without any contradiction, the four motifs of total depravity, salvation by grace, human responsibility, and the offer of salvation to all. Calvin and Luther's theology, on the other hand, can hold only the first two motifs together, and their doctrines of predestination and election explain why all will not be saved. Once again, the difference is important.

NOTES

[1] Outler, *Works,* 1:117. (*Salvation by Faith*)
[2] Ibid.
[3] Ibid., p. 98.
[4] Ibid., p. 260. (*The Spirit of Bondage and of Adoption*)
[5] Ibid., p. 117. (*Salvation by Faith*)
[6] Ibid., 2:388. (*God's Approbation of His Works*)
[7] Ibid., p. 175. (*Original Sin*)
[8] Ibid.
[9] Ibid., p. 177.
[10] Ibid., p. 178.
[11] Ibid., p. 176.
[12] Ibid., p. 185. (*Justification by Faith*); p. 212 (*The Righteousness of Faith*); p. 225 (*The Way to the Kingdom*); p. 403 (*Circumcision of the Heart*).
[13] Ibid., p. 184. (*Original Sin*)
[14] E. Gordon Rupp and Philip S. Watson, eds., *Luther and Erasmus: Free Will and Salvation* (Philadelphia: The Westminster Press, 1949), p. 266.
[15] John T. McNeill, *Calvin; Institutes of the Christian Religion,* 2 vols. (Philadelphia: The Westminster Press, 1960), 1:252.
[16] Outler, *Works,* 2:185. (*Original Sin*)
[17] Ibid., p. 184.
[18] Ibid., p. 185.
[19] Ibid.
[20] Ibid., p. 188.
[21] Ibid.
[22] Ibid., 3:207. (*On Working Out Our Own Salvation*)
[23] Ibid., 2:7. (*Original, Nature, Properties, and Use of the Law*)
[24] Ibid., 3:207. (*On Working Out Our Own Salvation*)
[25] Ibid., p. 545. (*Free Grace*)
[26] Paul M. Bassett and William M. Greathouse, *Exploring Christian Holiness, Vol. 2: The Historical Development,* (Kansas City: Beacon Hill Press, 1985), p. 210. Here from the sermon *On Working Out Our Own Salvation,* Greathouse draws out the idea that the natural state is a logical abstraction, but then applies it mistakenly to the natural state as employed in the sermon *On the Spirit of Bondage and of Adoption.*
[27] Outler, *Works,* 2:176. (*Original Sin*)
[28] Ibid., 1:142-43. (*Awake, Thou That Sleepest*)
[29] Ibid., pp. 263-65. (*The Spirit of Bondage and of Adoption*)

II

CONVINCING GRACE
AND INITIAL REPENTANCE

CONVINCING GRACE

In his lifetime, John Wesley traveled over 200,000 miles on horseback and preached literally thousands of sermons exhorting his hearers, among other things, to repent and "to flee from the wrath to come." This leader of Methodism was, therefore, unlike many of the more fashionable Anglican preachers of his day, for he was a sober, serious, and earnest preacher. Indeed, in the sermons delivered over the course of his life, John Wesley aimed not at popularity but at conviction of sin. He was not a smooth preacher who attempted to comfort people in their sins through flattery or other means. Instead, he often brought an uncomfortable and disturbing word to his listeners in order to assist them to realize their awful condition of life without God. Not surprisingly, conviction of sin is clearly the aim in several of his Standard Sermons.

In his sermon *Upon Our Lord's Sermon on the Mount: Discourse Eleven,* for example, produced in 1750, Wesley attempts to arouse the spiritual sensibilities of his congregation by pointing out the subtlety and insidious nature of sin. Sin is not what it appears to be, Wesley cautions, and it often masquerades as the good. Furthermore, this broad way, the way of disobedience to God's commandments as opposed to the narrow way of universal holiness, is inviting precisely because it is broad.[1] Wesley writes:

> And the very reason why many of these go on so securely in the "broad way" is because it is broad; not

considering that this is the inseparable property of the way
of destruction. . . . [And] while so few are found in the
way of life, and so many in the way of destruction, there is
great danger lest the torrent of example should bear us
away with them.[2]

Wesley then exhorts the people to depart from iniquity and
common example, and to walk henceforth in the straight and
narrow paths of God.

✳ It should be noted that whenever Wesley endeavors to stir
the conscience in his Standard Sermons, he usually has two
major groups in mind: first, "the vulgar herd, the poor, base,
stupid part of mankind,"[3] and second, interestingly, "the men
of eminence in the world,"[4] those who appear outwardly fair:
the wise, the rich, and the powerful. Although during the
revival, Wesley preached most often to the former, he was
conscious that the eminent and noble of this world, because of
their presumption and vanity, needed to hear the gospel perhaps
most of all. The sermons *The Almost Christian* and *Scriptural
Christianity* mark two of his attempts, among a few others, to
display the gospel before the venerable.

In *The Almost Christian,* preached at St. Mary's, Oxford,
on 25 July 1741, Wesley is in earnest to communicate the
difference between nominal Christianity and real Christianity.
This is because he believed that several of Oxford's ministers,
faculty, and students suffered under an illusion concerning their
true spiritual state. To dispel such deception, Wesley points out
the characteristics which make for an almost Christian and
which make for a real one. An almost Christian, he writes, is
marked first of all by a heathen honesty which avoids all of the
following: robbery, oppression of the poor, extortion, cheating,
and defrauding people of their rights. Almost Christians neither
forswear themselves nor do they slander others.[5] Second,
almost Christians have a form of godliness, all the external
markings of real Christians which are prescribed in the gospel
of Christ.[6] As such, they do nothing which the gospel
prohibits, but use all the means of grace at their disposal by
reading the Scriptures, frequenting the Table of the Lord, and
by using family prayer. Lastly, almost Christians are typified by
sincerity, by a real, inward principle of religion from which all
outward actions flow.[7]

On the other hand, it is in the latter part of this same
sermon that Wesley shows what is entailed in being an

altogether Christian. In addition to common virtue and reason-
ableness, altogether Christians are characterized, first of all, by
the love of God and, second, by the love of neighbor. This two-
fold love is established in the heart by neither sincerity nor zeal
but by faith alone. It is only the person who believes and trusts
in God who is truly free to love. Wesley elaborates:

> There is yet one thing more that may be separately
> considered, though it cannot actually be separate from the
> preceding, which is implied in the being "altogether a
> Christian" and that is the ground of all, even faith. . . . But
> here let no man deceive his own soul. It is diligently to be
> noted, the "faith which bringeth not forth repentance" and
> love, and all good works, is not that "right living faith"
> which is here spoken of, "but a dead devilish one. . . ."[8]

Certainly, some might argue even today that John Wesley
took great liberty in his sermon *The Almost Christian* by
presuming that his Oxford audience in July 1741 was composed
largely of nominal Christians. But suspicion existed on both
sides, and shortly before he delivered this homily, Wesley was
informed by John Gambold, an early Methodist turned Moravian, that he would not be well received.[9] Yet this sermon was,
after all, mild in comparison to what was to follow. Indeed, on
24 August 1744, Wesley delivered what was to be his last
installment before an Oxford congregation. If the previous
sermon, *The Almost Christian* had been warm in its exhortation
and convicting power, this last one, *Scriptural Christianity* was
outright hot. Here, after a brief delineation of the growth of
Christianity throughout history, Wesley issues a sweeping
indictment that moves from the general to the particular by
means of a number of pointed questions:

> With what propriety can we term any a Christian
> country which does not answer this description? . . . Is this
> city a Christian city? Is Christianity, scriptural Christianity,
> found here? . . . Are all the magistrates, all heads and
> governors of colleges and halls, and their respective
> societies (not to speak of the inhabitants of the town), "of
> one heart and of one soul"? . . . Are ye lively portraitures
> of him whom ye are appointed to represent among men?
> . . . Is this the general character of fellows of colleges? . . .
> Once more: what shall we say concerning the youth of this

place? Have you either the form or the power of Christian godliness?[10]

And Wesley concludes his various charges set in the form of questions with a climactic note; he accuses the youth assembled there of being "a generation of triflers; triflers with God, with one another, and with [their] own souls."[11] Little wonder this was his last address at Oxford.

Similarly, Charles Wesley had probed the conscience of Oxford two years earlier by means of a series of stinging questions in his sermon *Awake, Thou That Sleepest*. "Canst thou stand in his sight, 'who is of purer eyes than to behold iniquity?'"[12] "Hast thou recovered the image of God? . . . Hast thou put off the old man and put on the new?"[13] Finally, he inquires whether the elite of Oxford have received the Holy Ghost and have the witness in themselves.[14] Clearly, Charles Wesley hoped, like his brother John, that in all his queries his listeners would hear the voice of God calling them to repentance and that they would "feel that hammer of the Word which 'breaketh the rock in pieces.'"[15]

To be sure, one of the dominant motifs evident in these Oxford sermons and others is the contrast between outward religion and a religion of the heart, outward ordinances and inward holiness. In a later sermon, for instance, John Wesley urges his people not to be content with any religion which falls short of promoting a renewal in heart and life, and which, consequently, fails to restore the image of God.[16] Moreover, Charles, in the sermon just cited, stresses the reception of the Spirit, and like his father Samuel before him, the inward witness. However, these emphases were not well appreciated by several members of the Anglican clergy who looked upon the growth of Methodism with dismay and labeled its leaders "enthusiasts," or to use contemporary language, "fanatics." But John Wesley, interestingly enough, turned the tables on his detractors by throwing the charge of enthusiasm back at them! In his piece *The Nature of Enthusiasm* he rebuts:

> The first sort of enthusiasm which I shall mention is that of those who imagine they have the grace which they have not. Thus some imagine, when it is not so, that they have "redemption" through Christ, "even the forgiveness of sin" . . . This is properly an instance of the first sort of enthusiasm; it is a kind of madness, arising from the

imagination that they have that grace which in truth they have not; so that they only deceive their own souls.[17]

In light of the preceding, an important ingredient of at least some types of "enthusiasm" is presumption. Therefore, enthusiasts are also composed of those who assume they possess the grace and gifts which, in fact, they do not. And Wesley thought the most common type are those who imagine themselves Christians but are mistaken.[18] Therefore, orthodoxy, right opinions, belonging to an excellent church, doing no harm, and using all the means of grace are sheer vanity if they do not result in that change of heart characterized by love, peace, and joy in the Holy Spirit. In other words, real enthusiasm is not an emphasis on inward, spiritual renewal, as some of the clergy and even bishops of the Church of England had claimed to the detriment of the Wesleys, but is, quite simply, nominal Christianity.[19] John Wesley had turned the tables indeed.

Moral Law

Whenever Wesley designed to probe the conscience and to arouse conviction of sin, the Word of God, more specifically the moral law, was always close at hand. For instance, in his instructions to his lay preachers on preaching Christ, written in 1751, Wesley makes the moral law both the initial and the chief vehicle for convincing sinners:

> I think, the right method of preaching is this: At our first beginning to preach at any place, after a general declaration of the love of God to sinners, and his willingness that they should be saved, to preach the law, in the strongest, the closest, the most searching manner possible; only intermixing the gospel here and there, and showing it, as it were, afar off.[20]

But what is it exactly about the moral law that makes it such a suitable device for the manifestation of God's convincing grace? The answer is found in the very nature of this law. In his sermon *The Original, Nature, Property and Use of the Law*, Wesley describes the essential character of the moral law in two key ways. First of all, the law is "An incorruptible picture of the high and holy One that inhabiteth eternity. It is he whom in his essence no man hath seen or can see, made visible to men and angels."[21] It is the face of God unveiled; God revealed to his creatures as they are able to bear it.[22] It is the heart of God disclosed to humanity, the streaming forth or outbeaming of his glory, the express image of his person.[23] In addition, the law of God is a copy of the eternal mind, a transcript of the divine nature, and the fairest offspring of the everlasting Father.[24]

In a certain sense, all of the preceding descriptions are reminiscent of Plato's theory of forms as expressed in *The Republic*.[25] That is, just as human courage, according to Plato, is a shadowy approximation of ideal courage, so too the moral law, according to Wesley, is a shadow, a picture of God as humanity is able to bear it. In other words, because humanity is fallen and steeped in the darkness of sin, the immediate sight of the surpassing splendor of God would be overwhelming and devastating. Therefore, God clothes His splendor in the moral law, a vehicle which humans are able to bear. But even this accommodation to human weakness, clothed as it is, is able to spark terror and guilt in the sinner through the agency of the Holy Spirit, thus indicating its tremendous convicting power.

Second, Wesley expresses the nature of the law in terms of the created order. The moral law, he states, is "supreme, unchangeable reason; it is unalterable rectitude; it is the everlasting fitness of all things that are or ever were created."[26] This means, of course, that the law is in some sense reflective of the pristine beauty of the original state of creation; it is harmonious with the order and relations among things that God originally established there. It is like a mirror which reflects both the everlasting righteousness of God and the original righteousness of humanity.[27] In the moral law, then, Wesley had a standard to which he could appeal when the onslaught of sin wreaked such confusion in the lives of his hearers that they could no longer properly distinguish good from evil, and were, instead, led astray by every fad and opinion.

Not only does the nature of the law point to its convicting power, but the employment of moral law as a guide and spiritual catalyst does as well. In his major sermon on the use of the law, Wesley lists three main functions for this spiritual device.[28] However, properly speaking, it is only the first which expresses a strong accusatory force. Wesley states:

> And the first use of [moral law], without question, is to convince the world of sin. This is indeed the peculiar work of the Holy Ghost, who can work it without any

means at all, or by whatever means it pleaseth him . . . But
it is the ordinary method of the Spirit of God to convict
sinners by the law. It is this which, being set home on the
conscience, generally breaketh the rocks in pieces.[29]

In addition, Wesley affirms that the purpose of the first use of
the law is to destroy the life and strength wherein sinners
trust[30]—to shatter all manner of self-satisfaction—and to
convince them that they are spiritually dead while they live.[31]
Its function is, in short, to drive the sinner to Christ.

INITIAL REPENTANCE

A glimpse of the high and holy One who inhabits eternity,
a realization of the vast moral difference between Creator and
creature, and an acute awareness of human sin and frailty—all
of which are provided by the moral law—have the effect in
many cases of shocking the conscience and eventually leading
the sinner to repentance. As used here, the word "repent"
means to have a change of mind or heart, a conception that
Wesley maintains as well. But in his sermon *The Way to the
Kingdom* he views repentance principally in terms of self-
knowledge as evidenced by his admonition, "And first, repent,
that is know yourselves. This is the first repentance, previous to
faith, even conviction, or self-knowledge."[32] Such knowledge
makes people deeply sensible of their helplessness, guilt, and
sinfulness in the sight of a holy God. Wesley declares:

Know thyself to be a sinner, and what manner of
sinner thou art. Know that corruption of thy inmost
nature, whereby thou art very far gone from original
righteousness, whereby the flesh lusteth always contrary to
the Spirit . . . Know that thou art corrupted in every
power, in every faculty of the soul. . . .[33]

In other words, when the veil of self-deception is removed,
when no illusions concerning the essential goodness of the self
are tolerated, it is then that sinners gain an appreciation of their
true condition.

Although the sermon *The Way to the Kingdom,* preached in
1746, is one of the best windows through which to view
Wesley's understanding of repentance, it is largely lacking
concerning the emotional and psychological dynamics entailed

in this process. On the other hand, the homily *Upon Our Lord's Sermon on the Mount: Discourse One* is rich in detail with respect to those tempers and characteristics of spirit which often accompany repentance. "Real Christianity," Wesley notes in this latter sermon, "begins in poverty of spirit."[34] And though he observes that this poorness of spirit is "at all times found in a greater or less degree in every real Christian,"[35] Wesley nevertheless strongly associates it with the initial stage of repentance, as illustrated by the following: "Who then are the 'poor in spirit'? Without question, the humble; they who know themselves, who are convinced of sin; those to whom God hath given that first repentance which is previous to faith in Christ."[36] Poverty of spirit, then, which is so intimately associated with repentance, is the base upon which the whole fabric of Christianity is built; it is, in the words of Wesley, "the foundation of all"[37] and the first step to real substantial happiness.[38]

It should be noted, however, that Wesley distinguished two kinds of repentance. The first, or initial repentance, which has already been described above, is termed "legal" and entails a thorough conviction of sin. The second, or subsequent repentance, involves a change of heart from all sin to all holiness.[39] The former is concerned with actual sin, the latter with inbred or original sin.

The Means of Grace

What are convicted, repentant sinners to do in the meantime who hunger and thirst after righteousness, but who know themselves to be yet short of God's justifying grace? Should they use the means of grace and attend to the ordinances of the church, or should they instead do nothing and simply wait for faith? Again, will their works in any way detract from or— worse yet—spoil the chance for faith? These are some of the important questions which were addressed by Wesley in his sermon *The Means of Grace*. But before the major points of this sermon can be considered, some historical background is necessary in order to see how the central argument of this piece grew out of reflection on a difficult, real-life situation in the church. Here, therefore, is what should prove to be—like so many of Wesley's Standard Sermons—another fine instance of practical theology.

In the autumn of 1739, while Wesley was engaged in evangelistic work in Bristol, a certain Mr. Bray, a Moravian, began to disrupt the joint Methodist/Moravian Fetter Lane Society in London by teaching the congregation that it was unnecessary—even dangerous—to do outward works, that it was foolish to follow the ordinances of the church such as attending services and receiving the Lord's Supper, and that the congregation should "be still" before the Lord.[40] In November 1739, Philip Henry Molther, the private tutor of Count Zinzendorf's son, affirmed the teaching of Mr. Bray and convinced one of the women of the Fetter Lane Society that "she never had any faith at all; and . . . till she received faith [she should be] still," ceasing from outward works.[41]

After hearing these reports and after he interviewed Mr. Molther himself, Wesley was convinced that the Moravians were teaching errors. Moreover, when he saw the effect which these teachings had on the life of the congregation (many were leaving off good works and neglecting the ordinances of the church in order "to increase faith"), he took corrective action by expounding the Epistle of St. James and by teaching forthrightly the importance and necessity of the means of grace as continuing practices in the Christian life.

In the sermon *The Means of Grace,* which was not produced until a few years later in 1746, Wesley defines his topic in the following way: "By 'means of grace' I understand outward signs, words, or actions ordained of God, and appointed for this end—to be the *ordinary* channels whereby he might convey to men preventing, justifying, or sanctifying grace.[42]

Although Wesley distinguished two broad types of means, the instituted and the prudential, as reflected in the *Minutes of Several Conversations,*[43] he is concerned only with the former in this present sermon. In addition, of the five instituted means enumerated in the *Minutes* such as prayer, searching the Scriptures, receiving the Lord's Supper, fasting, and Christian conference, only the first three find their way into Wesley's homily.

The first means of grace to which Wesley directs the attention of all those who look to him for spiritual guidance is prayer. In this sermon, *The Means of Grace,* Wesley instructs his hearers to wait for the grace of God in the way of petition and intercession, in the path of prayer, both public and private.[44] And he observes that it is the Lord Himself who on a number of occasions taught the disciples and others the importance of communication with God and its absolute necessity in order to receive any gift from the Creator.

Second, Wesley urges those who are in earnest to be conformed to the image and likeness of God to search the Scriptures as a way to receive God's further grace and blessing. Through this second spiritual discipline, he notes, God not only "confirms and increases true wisdom"[45] in us, but also reproves, corrects, and instructs in righteousness "to the end 'that the man of God may be perfect, thoroughly furnished unto all good works.' "[46]

Lastly, Wesley preaches that all who desire spiritual growth and maturation are to wait for it, not passively but actively, especially in partaking of the Lord's Supper—a sacramental view which, by the way, clearly separates him from the Reformed tradition. To be sure, the Lord's Table in Wesley's thought is not restricted to professing Christians who know their sins to be forgiven through the merit of Christ's death, but is open to all who do truly repent and are heartily sorry for their sins. In a real sense, Wesley viewed the Lord's Supper as a converting ordinance, a means through which God's justifying grace could be bestowed upon the repentant sinner.[47]

In his doctrine of the means of grace, then, Wesley is able to affirm the appropriateness of these spiritual vehicles at any point in the spiritual journey of the individual. If one is not yet justified, the means are nevertheless important as the ordinary channels or conduits through which both the prevenient and sanctifying grace of God can flow. In other words, one is to wait for the further grace of God which brings salvation precisely by using these means and not by laying them aside. Indeed, it is, according to Wesley, the height of fanaticism and enthusiasm to expect the end of religion—the renewal of heart and mind—without a proper employment of the means.[48]

But just as Wesley cautions against underestimating or devaluing the means of grace, so too he warns against overvaluing and inflating them, a situation which occurs when it is forgotten that they are, after all, means and not ends. He writes:

> As to the manner of using them . . . it behoves us, first, always to retain a lively sense that God is above all means. . . . Secondly, before you use any means let it be deeply impressed on your soul: There is no power in this.

It is in itself a poor, dead, empty thing: separate from God, it is a dry leaf, a shadow. . . . Thirdly, in using all means, seek God alone.[49]

Moreover, Wesley reasons that when the means of grace are properly used, they neither detract from the graciousness of God nor do they accrue merit for their users.

What, then, are repentant, convicted sinners to do as they wait for the further grace of God which will result in justification? In his homiletical theology, Wesley answered emphatically that they are to employ all the means of grace at their disposal; they are to be active, not passive, ever improving the grace of God already received.

NOTES

[1] Outler, *Works,* 1:665. (*Sermon on the Mount, XI*)

[2] Ibid., pp. 668–69.

[3] Ibid., p. 667.

[4] Ibid.

[5] Ibid., p. 132. (*The Almost Christian*)

[6] Ibid.

[7] Ibid., p. 134.

[8] Ibid., p. 138.

[9] Ibid., p. 111. (*Salvation by Faith*)

[10] Ibid., pp. 173–78. (*Scriptural Christianity*)

[11] Ibid., p. 179.

[12] Ibid., pp. 148–49. (*Awake, Thou That Sleepest*)

[13] Ibid., p. 149.

[14] Ibid.

[15] Ibid., p. 152.

[16] Ibid., p. 697. (*Sermon on the Mount, XIII*)

[17] Ibid., 2:50–51. (*The Nature of Enthusiasm*)

[18] Ibid., p. 51.

[19] Ibid., p. 60. And see Outler's comments in the introduction to *The Nature of Enthusiasm,* p. 45.

[20] Thomas Jackson, ed., *The Works of John Wesley,* 14 vols. (Grand Rapids: Baker Book House, 1978), 11:486. (Letter on preaching Christ, 20 December 1751)

[21] Outler, *Works,* 2:9. (*Original, Nature, Properties, and Use of the Law*)

[22] Ibid.

[23] Ibid.

[24] Ibid., p. 10.

25This also reminds one of Plato's discussion of "ideas" and their earthly copies as found in the *Phaedrus*. In fact, Wesley even quotes from this work in the sermon. See M. A. Jowett, *The Dialogues of Plato*, 2 vols. (New York: Random House, 1937), 1:254.

26Outler, *Works*, 2:13. (*Original, Nature, Properties, and Use of the Law*)

27It should be noted that although Wesley tied the moral law to the created order, he nevertheless rejected the notion of a natural theology since for him there could be no perception of the law of God by reason apart from prevenient or sanctifying grace. See Kenneth J. Collins, "John Wesley's Theology of Law" (Ph.D. dissertation, Drew University, 1984), p. 62.

28Compare with Luther's uses of the law. Cf. Jaroslav Pelikan, ed., *Luther's Works*, 55 vols., Vol. 26: *Lectures on Galatians 1535* (Saint Louis: Concordia Publishing House, 1963), pp. 308f. Compare also with Calvin. Cf. John T. McNeill, ed., *Calvin: Institutes of the Christian Religion*, 2 vols. (Philadelphia: The Westminster Press, 1960), 1:360f.

29Outler, *Works*, 2:15. (*Original, Nature, Properties, and Use of the Law*)

30Ibid., p. 16.

31Ibid.

32Ibid., 1:225. (*The Way to the Kingdom*)

33Ibid.

34Ibid., p. 475. (*Sermon on the Mount, I*)

35Ibid.

36Ibid., p. 477.

37Ibid., p. 475.

38Ibid., p. 476. Note that Wesley specifically denies that the poor of which Jesus speaks in the Sermon on the Mount are to be understood in economic terms. However, Jose Bonino, a contemporary Methodist liberation theologian, has a difficult time understanding the poor as referred to by Jesus in any other way. Cf. Jose Miguez Bonino, *Doing Theology in a Revolutionary Situation* (Philadelphia: Fortress Press, 1975), pp. 112–14.

39John Wesley, *Explanatory Notes Upon the New Testament* (Salem, Ohio: Schmul Publishers), p. 15.

40Nehemiah Curnock, *The Journal of the Rev. John Wesley, A.M.*, 8 vols. (London: The Epworth Press, 1938), 2:312. See also, Kenneth J. Collins, "John Wesley and the Means of Grace," *The Drew Gateway* 56 (Spring 1986): 26–33.

41Ibid. (Bracketed material mine.)

42Outler, *Works*, 1:381. (*The Means of Grace*)

43Jackson, *Works*, 8:323.

44Outler, *Works*, 1:384. (*The Means of Grace*)

45Ibid., p. 387.

46Ibid., p. 388.

[47]Cf. *The Duty of Constant Communion,* Outler, *Works,* 3:427–39.
[48]Ibid., 2:56. (*The Nature of Enthusiasm*)
[49]Ibid., 1:395–96. (*The Means of Grace*)

III

JUSTIFICATION BY FAITH

WORKS PRECEDING JUSTIFICATION

Although Wesley recommended a judicious use of the means of grace prior to justification, he also affirmed that works which precede justification are not the basis for divine acceptance and approval. In his sermon *Salvation by Faith,* which was preached shortly after his Aldersgate experience, Wesley specifies in a way reminiscent of Anselm that all our works and righteousness prior to a vital faith in Christ merit nothing but condemnation.[1] This same assessment appears in the Journal of this period as well. Wesley declares, ". . .that my own works, my own sufferings, my own righteousness, are so far from reconciling me to an offended God, so far from making any atonement for the least of those sins . . . that the most specious of them need an atonement themselves, or they cannot abide His righteous judgement."[2]

To seek to be justified in God's sight through human works and by obedience to the law, therefore, is to proceed along a course that can issue only in frustration and failure. Wesley points out why this is so in his sermon *The Righteousness of Faith* in which he contends that the righteousness of the law involves an entire obedience to God, perfect in degree, and perfectly uninterrupted. In addition, it requires that humans should fulfill all righteousness, both inward and outward, negative and positive: that they should "abstain from every idle word, and avoid every evil work, [and] should keep every affection, every desire, every thought, in obedience to the will of God."[3] But this, according to Wesley, is clearly an impossibility for fallen humanity and should serve to show all the more clearly that the covenant of works, the righteousness based on law, which was given only to Adam in his unfallen state, was "never designed for the recovery of the favour and life of God once lost, but only for the continuance and increase thereof. . . ."[4]

The meritorious cause of justification, then, is not found in any sort of human ability or action, but in the life, ministry, and death of Jesus Christ who loved the world and gave His life for it. In other words, as Wesley observes, "the blood and righteousness of Christ, or (to express it a little more clearly) all that Christ hath done and suffered for us till he poured out his soul for the transgressors,"[5] is the sole foundation upon which people are made right with God. Notice here that Wesley does not limit the meritorious cause simply to the crucifixion of Christ, but instead includes the entire life and ministry of Jesus as an offering which is acceptable to God and which will issue in the justification of all who believe. This means, of course, that Wesley joins together both the passive righteousness (cru-cifixion) of Christ and his active righteousness (life and ministry), and it is with regard to both of these aspects that Wesley refers to Christ as "the Lord Our Righteousness."[6]

FAITH

But even if those who are spiritually concerned are sufficiently aware of the immense distance between their own unrighteousness and the righteousness of God, and also of the futility of their own works to establish a right relation with God, this in and of itself does not lead to justification of the sinner. In a real sense, Wesley sees the righteousness of Christ, indeed the Atonement, as something external to sinners, but which can result in their justification if it is appropriated. But how is such a benefit to be received? Upon what condition is the sinner, after all, to be justified? These are questions that were thoroughly explored by Wesley in his preached theology.

In a sermon expounded in the middle of his career, *The Scripture Way of Salvation,* Wesley proclaims that faith is the condition, and the only condition, of justification.[7] In other words, faith is both necessary and sufficient to justify the believer. It is necessary in the sense that no justification takes place without it. It is sufficient in the sense that justification occurs even if only faith is present. In Wesley's own words, "Everyone that believes is justified, whatever else he has or has not."[8] And this is exactly the same doctrine that Wesley preached in 1738 in his sermon *Salvation By Faith*.[9] The continuity is striking.

A remarkable difference, however, between these two sermons just cited is that *The Scripture Way of Salvation* is more cautious in its consideration of the place of works prior to justification. This concern most probably grew out of Wesley's rejection of Moravian quietism that was rampant in the joint Moravian/Methodist Fetter Lane society in 1740. To be sure, this sermon, as indicated earlier, maintains that faith is the only condition of salvation, but it then proceeds to indicate that repentance and fruits meet for repentance such as works of charity or mercy—and, one might add, the means of grace— are in some sense necessary to justification, if there be time and opportunity. Does this view, then, detract in any way from Wesley's earlier statements on this important subject? It does not, mainly because Wesley draws a tight distinction in this later sermon, a distinction, by the way, that was not always appreciated by his detractors. Wesley declares:

> God does undoubtedly command us both to repent and to bring forth fruits meet for repentance; which if we willingly neglect we cannot reasonably expect to be justified at all. Therefore both repentance and fruits meet for repentance are in some sense necessary to justification. But they are not necessary in the same sense with faith, nor in the same degree. Not in the same degree; for those fruits are only necessary conditionally, if there be time and opportunity for them. . . . Not in the same sense: for repentance and it fruits are only remotely necessary, necessary in order to faith; whereas faith is immediately and directly necessary to justification.[10]

That works are not necessary in the same degree as faith is exemplified in the Lukan account (23:43) of the thief on the cross who, quite obviously, did not have opportunity to perform works meet for repentance, but was nevertheless justified by faith in Christ. That works are not necessary in the same sense as faith highlights, for Wesley, the fact that such works are the normal prelude to justifying faith, and are done in response to the prevenient and convincing grace of God. There is no trace of merit here.

Albert Outler is certainly correct when he states that Wesley always believed the doctrine of justification by faith.[11] Indeed, Wesley, being the good Anglican that he was, would have come in contact with it through his use of *The Book of Common Prayer* and through *The Homilies* and the Anglican Thirty-nine Articles of Religion, just to name a few sources.[12] Moreover, Outler maintains that by the time Wesley returned to England from his missionary work in Georgia "the substance of his theology was already in his head . . . very little new doctrine was thereafter added or lost."[13] Once again, Outler works well with the primary evidence. But why then did Wesley write in 1772 that he did not clearly see that we are saved by faith until the year 1738?[14] And why did he maintain in his sermon *The Lord Our Righteousness,* preached in 1765, that the doctrine of justification by faith alone was one that he constantly believed and taught for almost twenty-eight years?[15] Again, the reference is to 1738. How can the seemingly contradictory notions that Wesley both knew and did not know this doctrine prior to 1738 be reconciled?

This apparent discrepancy is perhaps best explained by realizing that the verb "to know" functions on a number of different levels for Wesley. In one sense, a doctrine can be known intellectually so that one can recite the major tenets thereof. Wesley clearly had this kind of knowledge before 1738. Neither Peter Böhler nor August Spangenburg taught him this. Secondly, a doctrine such as justification by faith can also be known on a deeper, more experiential level, a level that Wesley, by his own admission, did not fully appreciate until 1738. In other words, although Wesley knew the doctrine of justification by faith from his youth, he had misunderstood *the nature* of that faith by which one is justified. In substantiation of this thesis, it should be noted that when Wesley later recalled his understanding of faith in 1725 and following, he wrote that he "was equally ignorant of *the nature* of saving faith; apprehending it to mean no more than a 'firm assent to all the propositions contained in the Old and New Testaments.' "[16] Moreover, in a stinging letter to William Law dated 14 May 1738, Wesley writes, "I know that I had not faith, unless the faith of a devil, the faith of Judas, that speculative, notional, airy shadow, which lives in the head, not in the heart. But what is this to the living, justifying faith in the blood of Jesus?"[17]

If Peter Böhler did not teach Wesley the doctrine of justification by faith, perhaps he was the one who introduced him to the experiential aspects of this doctrine by explaining the nature of faith completely and in a manner that was truly novel to Wesley. But this too is a difficult thesis to maintain, for one must take into account that on 29 January 1738, nine days before Wesley met Böhler at the house of Mr. Weinantz, he had recorded in his Journal material that clearly shows he already had a significant, though by no means thorough, understanding of the nature of the faith that he desired:

> The faith I want is "a sure trust and confidence in God, that, through the merits of Christ, my sins are forgiven, and I reconciled to the favor of God . . . I want that faith which none can have without knowing that he hath it; for whosoever hath it, is 'freed from sin, the' whole 'body of sin is destroyed' in him. . . ."[18]

What then was Böhler's chief contribution, if any, to Wesley's understanding of faith? It seems that Böhler filled out Wesley's knowledge of the nature of faith in an indirect way by stressing the fruits that necessarily flow from true faith. The two fruits inseparably associated with vital faith, Böhler argued, are dominion over sin and constant peace from a sense of forgiveness.[19] And it is this contribution that Wesley referred to as "new."[20] Therefore, on the one hand, to contend either that Böhler taught Wesley the doctrine of justification by faith or that he alone informed him of its nature is to ignore important evidence to the contrary. On the other hand, to maintain that Wesley completely comprehended the nature of faith prior to his encounter with Böhler is also an impossible position. Wesley both knew and did not know this vital doctrine before 1738. Böhler's contribution was important, but it was not total.[21]

In light of the preceding discussion, it should come as no surprise to learn that Wesley labored over the essential nature of faith in his Standard Sermons. In *Salvation by Faith,* for instance, which was preached days after his Aldersgate experience and before a congregation at St. Mary's, Oxford, Wesley's first point is under the head, "What faith it is through which we are saved."[22] And he, at least initially, answers this question along the lines of a *via negativa,* that is, Wesley informs his listeners what faith is *not* precisely so that they may gain a greater appreciation of what it is. And it is, first of all, not simply the faith of a heathen. The faith which justifies goes beyond the mere belief that God exists and that He rewards those who diligently seek Him. It also surpasses the knowledge of the being and attributes of God and a vigorous practice of moral virtue. In addition, it exceeds glorifying God by giving Him thanks for all good things. All of this, as noble as it may seem, is simply the faith of a Greek or a Roman, the faith of a heathen.[23]

Second, the faith through which one is saved is not that of a devil. According to Wesley, devils believe that "there is a wise and powerful God, gracious to reward and just to punish."[24] They also believe that "all Scripture was given by inspiration of God."[25] And so mere assent to all that is contained in the Bible, likewise, does not redeem. But the faith of a devil goes even beyond this to affirm, interestingly, that Jesus is the Son of God, even the Christ. Why, then, does not this latter faith save? Because it is cold and speculative. These evil spirits, being the great enemies of The Most High that they are, tremble in believing. They know that they are out of harmony with divine order and that someday they will be judged. Their faith is utterly encased in fear. They neither love this God they know nor are they willing to submit to His rule, and they have none of the holy tempers that characterize vital faith.

Third, to take this one step higher, justifying faith is not barely that which the apostles had while Christ was upon earth. Wesley maintains that even though the apostles left all to follow Jesus, healed the sick, and cast out devils, they were yet referred to by Christ as a "faithless generation."[26] How is this teaching to be understood? In a real sense, Wesley sees the apostles as transitional figures whose experience was unique, for they believed in Christ both before and after His death and resurrection. And it is precisely this former faith of the apostles which is inferior to the faith of later Christians who are able to acknowledge the necessity and merit of Christ's death and the power of His resurrection. In short, the prerogatives of the latter far exceed those of the former.

If justifying faith, then, is not simply belief in the existence of God nor the practice of moral virtue nor an assent to all that the Scriptures contain nor the knowledge that Jesus is the Son of God, the Christ, nor even the faith of the apostles when Jesus was on earth, then what precisely is it? This litany of what faith is not, offered by Wesley, illuminates many of the false starts and dead ends that he wished to spare his hearers, and it is not without its purpose: it prepares the way for a consideration of what, in fact, vital faith is.

The faith through which salvation is received is, first of all, "faith in Christ—Christ, and God through Christ, are the proper object of it."[27] And this is what distinguishes it from the faith of a heathen. Indeed, Wesley confesses in his brief spiritual autobiography recounted in the preface to the description of his Aldersgate experience that earlier he did not fix this faith on its proper object; then he meant only faith in God, not faith in or through Christ.[28]

Moreover, real faith is different from that of a devil in that "it is not barely a speculative, rational thing, a cold, lifeless assent, a train of ideas in the head; but also a disposition of the heart.[29] Notice here that Wesley does not exclude an intellectual component to faith; he simply points out that this ingredient by itself is insufficient; it must be joined to a disposition of the heart. That is, the mind must inform the heart, and the heart must engage the mind; it is both/and, not either/or.

Lastly, justifying faith goes beyond that of the apostles while Christ was on earth in that "it acknowledges the necessity and merit of his death, and the power of his resurrection."[30] This faith looks to the death of Christ as the only sufficient means of redeeming humanity from eternal death, and to his resurrection as the restoration of humanity to life and immortality.[31] In Wesley's own words, Christian faith is:

> . . . not only an assent to the whole gospel of Christ, but also a full reliance on the blood of Christ, a trust in the merits of his life, death, and resurrection; a recumbency upon him as our atonement and our life, as *given for us,* and *living in us.*It is a sure confidence which a man hath in God, that through the merits of Christ *his* sins are forgiven, and *he* reconciled to the favour of God. . . .[32]

Ever sensitive to the spiritual condition of his congregations and to their prejudices, Wesley concludes this sermon noted above by entertaining some of the objections he probably heard in the various churches that had already excluded him from their pulpits.[33] One such charge—that justification by faith alone will destroy the desire for both a holy life and good works—is refuted by Wesley in his observation that faith is not in opposition to holiness and good works, but is the only satisfactory means for their establishment. An emphasis on faith as the sole condition which is absolutely necessary for justification does not exclude either the holiness or the works that will necessarily flow from this faith—if, in fact, the faith is genuine. On the contrary, faith does not undermine the holy life, but creates and sustains it. Faith is not passive but is active in love and is the source, the dynamic power, behind holiness and good works.

To the charge that faith will make the holy law of God null and void, Wesley responds, ironically, that it is those who do not preach faith alone who actually overthrow the law because they exclude the only possible means for its performance and fulfillment. The height and depth of the law, the spiritual sense of it, is not diminished by faith, but is increased by it. Indeed, it is through one's relationship to Christ that one gains a greater, more profound, understanding of the law. The law sends one to Christ, to be sure, but Christ, according to Wesley, also sends one back to the law. The law is "the grand means whereby the blessed Spirit prepares the believer for larger communications of the life of God."[34]

The notion that God justifies freely by faith will encourage people to sin is another allegation which Wesley addresses. Now any gift of God may be abused and perverted by those who are unstable in mind (the enthusiasts) or who are not sincere. "But their blood is upon their own head,"[35] Wesley cautions; "the goodness of God ought to lead them to repentance."[36] But won't this teaching drive people to despair? Yes, Wesley affirms, it will cause them "to despair of being saved by their own works, their own merits or righteousness."[37] But this is a good and not an evil thing, and it illustrates the therapeutic nature of saving faith. The proper medicine may appear painful at first, but it has good lasting effects.

Moreover, when Anglican priests complained that surely this was an uncomfortable doctrine—probably because they did, in fact, realize that it would drive many people to despair and would overturn all human righteousness—Wesley replied in his homily by using their own tools against them. For in describing this faith, he quotes verbatim the phrase that it is "very full of comfort" from Article Eleven of the Thirty-nine Articles of Religion which reads:

> We are accounted righteous before God, only for the merit of our Lord and Saviour Jesus Christ by Faith, and not for our own works or deservings. Wherefore, that we are justified by Faith only, is a most wholesome Doctrine, and very full of comfort, as more largely is expressed in the Homily of Justification.[38]

The irony of all this, of course, is that Wesley was criticized for preaching both *sola fide* and *sola gratia* by a clergy that should have known better, if they were at all familiar with the standards of their own church.

Lastly, to the claim that this doctrine should not be preached at all, or at least not as the first doctrine, Wesley responds, "But what saith the Holy Ghost? Other foundation can no man lay than that which is laid, even Jesus Christ,"[39] and he continues, "so, then, 'that whosoever believeth on him shall be saved' is and must be the foundation of all our preaching; that is, must be preached first."[40] In addition, this is a doctrine, Wesley asserts, from which none are to be excluded. It is for the poor, the unlearned, the young, the sinner; indeed, for every creature under heaven. It is the strong rock and foundation of the Christian religion.[41]

JUSTIFICATION

As indicated above, it is of little profit simply to note that Wesley knew the doctrine of justification by faith prior to 1738. Few doubt that Wesley was familiar with the doctrinal standards of his own church which aptly express this teaching. Instead, what was the range and extent of Wesley's understanding of both faith and justification prior to this time? That is the important question. The question of faith has already been addressed; it is now time to consider justification.

As Wesley, by his own admission, was ignorant of the nature of faith prior to 1738, so too was he ignorant of the *nature* of justification. And his breakthrough concerning the essential nature of justification also came in 1738 as evidenced by his comment to John Newton in 1765: "I think on Justification just as I have done any time these seven-and-twenty years, and just as Mr. Calvin does. In this respect I do not differ from him a hair's breadth."[42] But before 1738, Wesley often confused justification with sanctification, that is, he often considered the holy life with its good works and earnestness as the basis of justification instead of as its fruit. In a real sense, Wesley was predisposed to such thinking by the contemporary understanding and practice of his own Anglican church. In a letter to William Green in 1739, for example, Wesley observes that the habit of the English clergy is to place sanctification before justification with the result that the holy life becomes the basis upon which one is justified.[43] That Wesley made this kind of error as well is revealed in a few of his autobiographical comments that emerge in his *Farther Appeal*:

> I was ordained Deacon in 1725, and Priest in the year following. But it was many years after this before I was convinced of the great truths above recited. During all that time I was utterly ignorant of *the nature* and condition of justification. Sometimes I confounded it with sanctification; (particularly when I was in Georgia).[44]

So, then, it is not denied that the language of *sola fide* and justification most certainly passed through the lips of John Wesley every time he took Communion and recited from the *Book of Common Prayer,* "We do not presume to come to this thy Table trusting in our own righteousness but in thy manifold and great mercies. . ."[45] However, the point is, if his Journal and Letters are to be given any weight, he had not properly digested the language that had so easily passed through his lips.

With this background in mind, it is not surprising to learn that Wesley takes great care in defining the nature of justification in his sermon *Justification by Faith.* Apparently, he wants to leave no room for misunderstanding concerning this significant teaching. And just as he defined the nature of faith earlier in terms of a *via negativa,* thereby removing most of the obstacles and much of the confusion surrounding it, so too he explores the nature of justification in this present sermon by pointing out precisely what it is not.

Justification, first of all, is not "the being made actually just and righteous. This is *sanctification*; which is indeed in some degree the immediate fruit of justification, but nevertheless is a distinct gift of God."[46] Wesley keeps these doctrines separate, conceptually if not in practice, by making a distinction between the work that God does for us (justification) and the work that

He does in us (sanctification). Elsewhere Wesley teaches that justification entails a relative change, but sanctification a real one: "The former changes our outward relation to God, so that of enemies we become children; by the latter our inmost souls are changed so that of sinners we become saints."[47] The one takes away the guilt of sin; the other removes its power.

Justification is also not the action of God that "[clears] us from the accusation brought against us by *the law*"[48] in the sense that "whereas we have transgressed the law of God . . . God does not inflict on those who are justified the punishment which they had deserved."[49] What Wesley is most probably trying to point out here—and this is a difficult passage—is that justification does not simply deal with the issue of punishment to the exclusion of a consideration of the actual transgression itself. To do so could result in antinomianism in the sense that God's justifying activity would be viewed as somehow entailing a license to sin or, worse yet, to remain comfortable in sin since all penalty has been removed.

For Wesley, justification, quite simply, means pardon, the forgiveness of past sins. "It is that act of God the Father," he asserts, "whereby, for the sake of the propitiation made by the blood of his Son, he 'showeth forth his righteousness by the remission of sins that are past.' "[50] Note that justification as used here presumes sin and is not prescribed for those who are already righteous, such as Adam in his pristine state. Instead, justification is the salutary way offered by God to a fallen people who earnestly seek the reestablishment of a right relationship with God. It is the healing balm for all unrighteousness, and the only way marked by God appropriate for the redemption of sinners.

But justification, Wesley insists, does not imply that "God is deceived in those whom he justifies; that he thinks them to be what in fact they are not."[51] God simply does not judge those who are justified contrary to the real nature of things nor does He confound them with Christ. With little doubt, when Wesley employed this kind of language, he had some of the Calvinistic Methodists in mind. For example, John Cennick and James Hervey championed a much broader concept of imputation than Wesley could allow, and which he feared would result in antinomianism, the neglect of God's holy law (God does not see my sin but only the righteousness of Christ). Does this mean, then, that Wesley denied that the righteousness of Christ is imputed to believers? Not at all, but his understanding—as will be shown below—was in sharp contrast to that of the Calvinistic Methodists.

In his sermon *The Lord Our Righteousness,* written in 1765 in response to a publication of Hervey's that was published posthumously, Wesley declares that the human righteousness of Christ, both internal and external, active and passive, is imputed to believers when they believe; "in that very hour the righteousness of Christ is theirs."[52] Indeed, faith and the righteousness of Christ are inseparable, and there is no true faith that does not have this righteousness as its object.[53] In these statements, at least, Wesley not only shows that he too has a doctrine of imputation, but that it is also similar in some respects to that held by his Calvinistic friends. Yet when he goes on to ask, "In what sense is the righteousness imputed to believers?"[54] some of the most significant differences between the two wings of Methodism begin to emerge.

For Wesley, the righteousness of Christ is imputed to believers in the sense that they are accepted by God not for the sake of anything that they have done, but solely because of what Christ has accomplished through His life and death on their behalf. In other words, Wesley's doctrine of imputation is another way of highlighting the *sola fide* and *sola gratia* aspects of justification by faith. "We are justified freely by his grace, through the redemption that is in Jesus Christ,"[55] Wesley declares. Here, therefore, imputation means that the righteousness of Christ is the "whole and sole meritorious cause of the justification of the sinner before God."[56] The Calvinistic Methodists, on the other hand, rejected Wesley's use of the phrase "meritorious cause," preferring to view the work of Christ as the "formal" cause of justification. The former phrase excludes the idea of predestination; the latter implies it.

But there are other differences to be sure. Wesley employed the language of imputation in his sermons so long as it was understood that it related only to justification, to forgiveness and acceptance, and not to sanctification. This fencing of the doctrine of imputation to keep it from flowing into the doctrine of sanctification expressed Wesley's concern and fear, especially after 1765, that imputation, improperly understood, could easily lead to taking the righteousness of Christ as a cloak for the sinner's own unrighteousness. Wesley writes:

In the meantime what we are afraid of is this: lest any should use the phrase, "the righteousness of Christ," or, "the righteousness of Christ is 'imputed to me,'" as a cover for his unrighteousness. . . . Warn them against making "Christ the minister of sin"! Against making void that solemn decree of God, "without holiness no man shall see the Lord," by a vain imagination of being holy in Christ. O warn them that if they remain unrighteous, the righteousness of Christ will profit them nothing![57]

Moreover, because of his fear of antinomianism, Wesley, at times, was unwilling to let the statement "the righteousness of Christ is imputed to believers" stand alone, but immediately added that "God implants righteousness in every one to whom he has imputed it."[58] In this line of thought, imputed righteousness (justification) is the ground of acceptance with God; inherent righteousness (sanctification) is the fruit of such acceptance. Thus, Wesley drew a relation between faith and holy living, justification and sanctification, and insisted that the latter must flow from the former. Furthermore, his concern for holy living, so evident in his sermon *The Lord Our Righteousness,* was in no way diminished either by his proclamation of justification by faith or by his promulgation of the imputation of the righteousness of Christ.

The picture which is beginning to emerge, then, is that although Wesley's doctrine of justification by faith does, indeed, have something in common with the Calvinist and Lutheran traditions in its emphasis upon *sola fide* and *sola gratia,* there are notable differences as well, especially in relation to the matter of imputation. Luther, for example, did not limit imputation to forgiveness and justification, as Wesley does, but included sanctification as well. In his *Lectures on Galatians,* for instance, this German Reformer noted, "On account of this faith in Christ God does not see the sin that still remains in me. For so long as I go on living in the flesh, there is certainly sin in me. But meanwhile Christ protects me under the shadow of His wings."[59] In a similar fashion, Calvin claimed that the believer is so clothed in the righteousness of Christ that he "appears in God's sight not as a sinner but as a righteous man,"[60] a formulation that Wesley specifically rejects.

But perhaps even Wesley's own claim that he thinks on justification "just as Mr. Calvin does" can be called into question. If one simply focuses on the doctrine of justification, not mindful of its theological context in terms of what both precedes and follows it in the order of salvation, then there is, indeed, some similarity between Wesley and Calvin (and Luther for that matter) in the sense that the law, and works of the law, play no role in the act of justification itself. But if one is attentive to the larger theological setting in which the respective doctrines of justification are placed, then much less similarity emerges.

It should not be forgotten, for example, nor taken lightly, that Wesley's doctrine of justification is preceded by divine/human cooperation (synergism) in the form of the prevenient grace of God which fosters human responsibility. This means that, for Wesley at least, people are in some sense responsible for whether or not they are justified (although they cannot justify themselves) since the universal and free prevenient grace of God which renders them accountable has already been given. This same concept of prevenient grace is also behind Wesley's different evaluation of the role and necessity of works prior to justifying faith, and his placing of repentance, for the most part, before justifying faith, not simultaneous with it, ideas that were clearly repudiated by the continental Reformers.

Simply put, Calvin's theological structure in the form of unconditional election, limited atonement, and irresistible grace, and Luther's structure in the form of predestination and determinism as expressed in his *De Servo Arbitrio* gave their respective doctrines of justification, despite Wesley's protests to the contrary, a flavor that was, after all, much different from his own.

EXCURSUS

ALBERT OUTLER AND ALDERSGATE: A REEVALUATION

Albert Outler, one of the leading contemporary Wesley scholars, has made several significant contributions to the field, especially in terms of assisting in the production of a critical edition of Wesley's Works, (although much work is yet to be done) and also in terms of galvanizing a more serious study of Wesley that looks beyond the popular images. He has stressed the importance of reading "the whole Wesley," that scholars must move beyond the 1730s and '40s and attempt to comprehend the mature Wesley with his subtle shifts in emphases, and he has reopened the question of Wesley as a significant theologian in his own right. But perhaps Outler's greatest contribution has been the attempt to break Wesley out of his Methodist cocoon so that not only will Wesley's genius in practical theology be fully appreciated in Methodism, but in other, quite diverse, traditions as well.

As great as his contributions are, Outler's handling of the primary sources and the interpretive models used to explain them, can in some instances be called into question. If scholarship in this area is to proceed not by dint of authority but by reason—and no doubt Outler would agree with this as well—then different models, other hermeneutical constructs, can and should be offered.

Therefore, let us take yet another look at Wesley's Aldersgate experience, this time in terms of Outler's treatment of it. Three major questions will be entertained: First, does reference to this experience really drop out of Wesley's writings shortly after it occurred? Second, does the spiritual frustration and depression that Wesley encountered after Aldersgate detract from or even eliminate the decisive nature of 24 May 1738? Third, is Aldersgate best understood simply in terms of the doctrine of assurance? It is to these questions that this work now turns.

Outler, first of all, attempts to downgrade the importance of 24 May 1738, by arguing that there is a "paucity of Wesley's own references to Aldersgate,"[61] and by maintaining that this experience was simply "one in a series of the turning points in [Wesley's] passage from don to missionary to evangelist."[62] But is this the only interpretation of the primary evidence that can be offered? Obviously not, for J. Ernest Rattenbury believes that Dr. Grant Cell has correctly discerned a chronology, a way of reckoning time in Wesley's writings that makes Aldersgate its center. Quoting Cell, Rattenbury writes, "In addition to the human way of timing events *Anno Domini*—there are scattered throughout the twenty-five volumes of his writings references, not a few cases, but numbered by the score to his conversion experience, *anno meae conversion is*."[63]

How can the evidence be handled so differently by Outler and Rattenbury, two very competent scholars, who, by the way, represent two of the major schools on this subject? Must they forever talk past one another? More importantly, does either of these theologians have an "agendum" in the form of unexpressed presuppositions and assumptions that prevents them from seeing what actually is in the text? In order to answer these rather difficult questions, a detailed examination of the evidence upon which these divergent views are based must be undertaken.

In Wesley's sermons, theological treatises, and letters there are some specific references to 24 May 1738, as well as some general references to the year 1738 that cannot be denied, although they have often been misunderstood. Indeed, the following pieces of evidence, numerous though by no means exhaustive, appear to support Rattenbury's claim that there truly is a distinct reckoning of time in the Wesleyan literature:

1. Four days after his Aldersgate experience Wesley told some friends at the house of Mr. Hutton that "five days before he was not a Christian."[64]

2. On 30 October 1738, John wrote to his older brother, Samuel, "By a Christian I mean one who so believes in Christ as that sin hath no more dominion over him. And in this obvious sense of the word I was not a Christian till May 24th last past."[65]

3. Wesley's comment in his Journal on 4 January 1739, which is frequently used to diminish the significance of May 24 actually supports it by referring specifically to that date. He writes, "My friends affirm I am mad, because I said I was not a Christian a year ago. . . .

Indeed, what I might have been I know not, had I been faithful to the grace then given. . . ."[66]

4. In a letter to "John Smith" on 30 December 1745, Wesley said, "For it is true that from May 24 1738, 'wherever I was desired to preach, salvation by faith was my only theme'. . . And it is equally true that 'it was for preaching the love of God and man that several of the clergy forbade me their pulpits' before that time, before May 24, before I either preached or knew salvation by faith."[67]

5. On 22 June 1740, Wesley wrote in one of his letters, "After we had wandered many years in the new path of salvation by faith and works, about *two* years ago it pleased God to show us the old way of salvation by faith only."[68]

6. In a lengthy letter to Thomas Church on 2 February 1745, Wesley repeated his claim put forth on 22 June 1740, just cited and added, "Let us go no farther, as to time, than seven years (1738) last past."[69]

7. Again in a letter to Thomas Church on 17 June 1746, Wesley traced the course of his ministry: "From the year 1725 I preached much, but saw no fruit of my labour. . . . From the year 1729 to 1734 . . . I saw a little fruit. . . . From 1734 to 1738 I saw more fruit of my preaching. . . . From 1738 to this time . . . the word of God ran as fire among the stubble."[70]

8. In 1765, Wesley wrote to John Newton, "I think on Justification just as I have done any time these seven-and-twenty years, and just as Mr. Calvin does."[71]

9. In that same year he wrote to Dr. Erskine, "In . . . justification by faith I have not wavered a moment for these seven-and-twenty years."[72]

10. In November 1765, in his sermon *The Lord Our Righteousness,* Wesley stated concerning justification by faith, "This is the doctrine which I have constantly believed and taught for *near* eight-and-twenty years. This I published to all the world in the year 1738. . . ."[73]

11. In 1772, Wesley observed, "With regard to [the doctrine] that we are justified merely for the sake of what Christ has done and suffered, I have constantly and earnestly maintained [that] above four and thirty years."[74]

12. Wesley affirmed in 1778, "I am not sensible that this has made any essential addition to my knowledge in divinity. Forty years ago I knew and preached every Christian doctrine (including justification by faith) which I preach now."[75] Once again, the reference is to 1738.[76]

Albert Outler is well aware of the pivotal nature of the year 1738 and all the material documented above, but he interprets the latter as evidence of the process of "Wesley's change from a faith in faith to faith itself, from aspiration to assurance,"[77] and argues that "the Aldersgate story as such drops abruptly out of sight after its publication in the second extract of the Rev. Mr. John Wesley's Journal (1740)."[78] But this last claim is obviously false in light of Wesley's correspondence with "John Smith" on 30 December 1745. To be sure, Wesley does in fact refer specifically to the Aldersgate experience on at least four occasions ranging from the year 1738 to 1745 (first four items above). After 1745, he repeatedly refers to the year 1738 throughout the course of his ministry and in a manner that warrants attention. In contrast to Outler's view, then, it can be argued, given the general nature of these later references, that Wesley just might have had 24 May 1738, in mind as he wrote this material. Such a view, far from being obscure, gains considerable support in light of Wesley's own precedent of highlighting the day of 24 May above all others in the year 1738. To argue, therefore, that this interpretation is impossible, that the later material unequivocally excludes reference to Aldersgate, as Outler does, is to claim to know too much. Indeed, it begs the question.

Second, Outler contends that the Aldersgate experience has been over-emphasized by noting that "before May 24 Wesley records moments of equal, or nearly equal, spiritual exaltation,"[79] and by arguing that "in the first six months after 'Aldersgate' [Wesley] reports numerous instances of acute spiritual depression, equal in severity to anything preceding."[80] Concerning the former issue, it must be asked why, if prior to

24 May Wesley really did record moments of equal spiritual exaltation and if he did not intend to stress the pivotal nature of this subsequent event and its dramatic impact, did he take the trouble in his Journal to offer a preface to the Aldersgate experience that recounted his spiritual biography up to that time? But even Outler must and, interestingly, does admit the drama of this account, and that the experiences of Paul and Augustine were "clearly in Wesley's mind"[81] when he wrote it. How, then, is this event equal to what has preceded?

Concerning the latter issue of Wesley's spiritual depression—that he was troubled by "those symptoms of spiritual unsettlement which real faith was supposed to remove"[82]—one must first of all understand the nature of this spiritual distress, the reason for its existence, and then, and only then, can some judgment be made with respect to its bearing upon the 24 May event. The mere citation of Wesley's more somber moods and his subsequent spiritual struggles, as for example on 4 January 1739, in itself proves nothing, for it must then be shown in what way and to what extent these experiences were inconsistent with or detracted from that of Aldersgate.

Just how is Wesley's spiritual condition shortly after Aldersgate—that, for example, he was described by the Moravians as *Homo Perturbatus*—best understood? A little background is necessary. It is a commonplace in Wesley studies that John Wesley saw the end or purpose of religion, which is holiness of heart and life, before he saw the proper means (faith) for its establishment. Indeed, Wesley was an earnest and sincere priest who knew the end of religion as far back as 1725–27 when he read the triumvirate of Law, à Kempis, and Taylor. Moreover, a few years later, in 1733, he wrote an important sermon on this subject, "The Circumcision of the Heart," in which one can find in his works no better or loftier description of the holy life. Now what kind of error is such a man yet likely to make once he realizes that faith, not works or moral endeavor, is the proper foundation of holiness? Perhaps, just perhaps, Wesley thought that the height and depth of the holy life that he had envisioned as far back as 1725 would be utterly realized in the act of saving faith. In substantiation of this hypothesis, note the connection that Wesley drew between the means and the end of religion in his Journal account on board the *Samuel* en route to England on 29 January 1738:

The faith I want is "a sure trust and confidence in God, that, through the merits of Christ, my sins are forgiven, and I reconciled to the favor of God" . . . I want that faith which none can have without knowing that he hath it; for whosoever hath it, is "freed from sin, the" *whole* "body of sin is destroyed" in him: he is freed from fear, "having peace with God through Christ, and rejoicing in hope of the glory of God."[83]

Could it be that Wesley's own spiritual turmoil after Aldersgate was precipitated, for the most part, by his painful realization that justifying faith neither destroys the whole body of sin (which must await the further work of entire sanctification) nor does it remove all manner of fear and the heaviness that results from manifold temptations? Again, was Wesley's experience similar to that of Christian David which Wesley saw fit to record in his Journal on 10 August 1738, in the following words:

I saw not then that the first promise to the children of God is, "Sin shall no more reign over you"; but thought I was to feel it in me no more from the time it was forgiven. Therefore, although I had the mastery over it, yet I often feared it was not forgiven, because it still stirred in me, and at some times thrust sore at me that I might fall: because, though it did not reign, it did remain in me; and I was continually tempted, though not overcome.[84]

Yet Outler remains unpersuaded. And so in a further attempt to downplay the importance of Aldersgate by highlighting Wesley's subsequent depression, which "real faith" was supposed to remove, he contends that there were several instances after 24 May 1738, when Wesley even denied that he was or ever had been a Christian.[85] In his book *John Wesley,* for example, Outler specifically refers the reader to a very dark though remarkably honest letter from John to his brother Charles in June 1766, part of which reads as follows:

In one of my last I was saying I do not feel the wrath of God abiding on me; nor can I believe it does. And yet (this is the mystery) [I do not love God. I never did.] Therefore [I never] believed in the Christian sense of the word. Therefore [I am only an] honest heathen, a proselyte of the Temple, one of the God-fearers.[86]

But how is such an obscure and unrepresentative passage to be interpreted? If one employs it as Outler does in order to debunk Aldersgate, then a question immediately emerges: Why stop there? At face value, the letter reveals that Wesley never was a Christian in 1738 or in 1725 or at any other time prior to 1766 for that matter. But does Outler, and those who follow in his train, really wish to claim *this?* Indeed, the difficulty of such an interpretation should indicate all the more clearly that the language of this letter is a fine instance of Wesley's tendency, on occasion, toward hyperbole pure and simple.

Now it is one thing to argue and to note correctly that there were times, after Aldersgate, when Wesley was dissatisfied with his spiritual walk. However, it is quite another thing to maintain, as Outler does, that this detracts from the crucial flavor of Aldersgate. Where in Wesley's writings (except in the evidence already cited) does he claim that the new birth cannot be followed by a measure of doubt, fear, or even depression? How, then, is such evidence cited against him? By way of implication, does Outler really wish to assert that regeneration cannot be followed by the kinds of feelings that Wesley in his candor displayed in his Journal? If this really is the case, then it is doubtful whether anyone at all could be deemed born of God since any subsequent negative evidence could be used to support the contrary.

One final issue in this area needs to be addressed. Those who view Aldersgate as John Wesley's experience of the new birth do *not* claim, as is erroneously charged, that prior to this event he was utterly without faith. Instead, it is observed that before May 1738 Wesley indeed had faith, but it was the faith of a servant, tinged with self-justification and fear, a legal faith, and not the faith of a son.[87] In other words, the sharpest contrast possible between pre- and post-Aldersgate experiences is not necessary for those scholars like Rattenbury and others who contend that the Journal account of 24 May basically chronicles Wesley's own regeneration.

Third, regarding Peter Böhler's advice to Wesley on 4 March 1738, that he should "Preach faith till you have it; and then, because you have it, you will preach faith,"[88] Outler writes, "That is, preach the doctrine of justification by faith (which Wesley had always believed) until he had the personal assurance of it."[89] To be sure, Outler prefers to view the Aldersgate experience which followed, not as Wesley's conversion to vital Christianity, but as the time when he moved from "faith in faith to faith itself, from aspiration to assurance."[90] But is an appeal to the doctrine of assurance sufficient to explain all that occurred on 24 May? Observe the many elements in Wesley's own account of Aldersgate:

> In the evening I went very unwillingly to a society in Aldersgate Street, where one was reading Luther's preface to the *Epistle to the Romans*. About a quarter before nine, while he was describing the change which God works in the heart through faith in Christ, I felt my heart strangely warmed. I felt I did trust in Christ, Christ alone for salvation; and an assurance was given me that He had taken away my sins, even mine, and saved me from the law of sin and death.[91]

Notice that Wesley connects a number of items in the selection above with the conjunction "and": trust in Christ alone, *and* assurance, *and* freedom from the law of sin and death. If there ever were a good example of Wesley's conjunctive theology which Outler is so fond of pointing out,[92] this is it. Therefore, it is certainly not denied that assurance is an integral part of a total picture; what is denied, however, is that assurance is the whole of Aldersgate. The reference to freedom from the law of sin and death—and trust in Christ alone for that matter—must neither be minimized nor repudiated in any assessment of this experience. And it is Wesley, himself, who first of all focused on this last aspect of power over sin, and not the Methodist hagiographers. Wesley considered such power to be a watershed in his spiritual walk, especially when he wrote continuing the account of Aldersgate: "And herein I found the difference between this and my former state chiefly consisted. I was striving, yea, fighting with all my might under the law, as well as under grace. But then I was sometimes, if not often, conquered; now, I was always conqueror."[93]

One will search Wesley's Journals and Diaries in vain for any description of this kind of spiritual power prior to May 1738. Instead, one finds statements that reveal Wesley's own acute awareness of sin, his inability to keep the holy law of God, and his utter failure to realize several of his ideals. In fact, prior to Aldersgate, Wesley described himself as one "under the law,"[94] and as desiring both salvation ("Our end in leaving our native country was . . . to save our souls. . . .")[95] and conversion ("I, who went to America to convert others, was never myself converted to God.") But note that Wesley added the remark, "I'm not sure of this."[96]

It is even more interesting when one makes a comparison between the major ingredients of the Aldersgate account and two of Wesley's sermons on the new birth, namely, *The Marks of the New Birth* and *The Great Privilege of the Children of God.* When this is done, it becomes apparent that the Journal account in May 1738 basically describes Wesley's own regeneration.[97] For this was the time when he exercised that faith which delivers from both the guilt and power of sin, when he had the hope which arises out of a sense of forgiveness, and when he was marked by the love of God and neighbor in a deeper way.

Therefore, when Outler writes that "Aldersgate was not the time when John Wesley became a 'real Christian,' "[98] one must ask in what sense this is to be understood. If "real Christian" means a call to the ministry, sincerity in spiritual life, and an earnestness displayed in missionary service, then Wesley, of course, was a Christian prior to May 1738. If, however, the phrase is understood in an evangelical way, as the time when one experiences both forgiveness and freedom from the guilt and power of sin plus the assurance which results from this, then by no stretch of the imagination was Wesley a Christian prior to Aldersgate. Moreover, that the latter definition is more appropriate to Wesley's own consideration of the matter is substantiated by the theology displayed in his Standard Sermons, especially in the pieces on the prerogatives of the children of God.

Why, then, is Outler still not persuaded? Perhaps because he, and other scholars like him, cannot fail to be impressed by the zeal of the early Wesley in his many activities on behalf of the church. But do these things count for salvation? Do works, earnestness, sincerity, and zeal make a Christian? Wesley thought not, and this is the key to his spiritual trajectory. Perhaps Outler has not fully considered the idea implicit in *sola fide,* that so much which matters can happen in such a short time, with the corollary that so much which does not matter can happen over a long period of time. But if salvation, hence being a real Christian, is by faith, then why not? Is Outler's theology predisposed to misprize brief, powerful, and significant crisis experiences? Indeed, Outler's argumentation, his attempt to deflate Aldersgate and its significance, reminds one of Mrs. Hutton's protestation in the face of Wesley's own claim on 28 May 1738, that five days earlier he was not a Christian: "If you was not a Christian ever since I knew you," she protested, "you was a great hypocrite, for you made us all believe you was one."[99]

Despite the new wave in Wesley studies, the importance of the Aldersgate account as a hermeneutical device through which one can gain insight into Wesley's spiritual dynamic cannot be denied. The dramatic structure of this account, the allusions to other significant conversion experiences within it, the spiritual autobiography which precedes it, and Wesley's own references to spiritual power and victory which conclude the record illustrate the fact that this was an extraordinary occurrence.

Moreover, the claim that reference to this experience simply drops out of Wesley's writings is subject to both question and interpretation. The appeal to the spiritual frustration and depression which Wesley encountered after 24 May can be understood in other ways which do not necessarily detract from this event. Nor is it salutary to trim the experience of its several ingredients and to highlight one aspect, namely, assurance. To be sure, much more happened at Aldersgate than simply assurance; it was the time when Wesley not only trusted in Christ, but when he also experienced freedom from both the guilt and power of sin. And when these various parts are considered together, none to the exclusion of the others, they indicate that Aldersgate was a crucial experience for Wesley after all.

NOTES

[1] Outler, *Works,* 1:126. (*Salvation By Faith*)
[2] Curnock, *Journal,* 1:423.
[3] Outler, *Works,* 1:204–05. (*The Righteousness of Faith*)
[4] Ibid., 1:210.
[5] Ibid., 2:157–58. (*The Scripture Way of Salvation*)
[6] Ibid., 1:453. (*The Lord Our Righteousness*)
[7] Ibid., 2:162. (*The Scripture Way of Salvation*)
[8] Ibid.
[9] Ibid., 1:118. (*Salvation by Faith*)
[10] Ibid., 2:162–63. (*The Scripture Way of Salvation*)
[11] Albert C. Outler, "Towards a Re-Appraisal of John Wesley as a Theologian," *The Perkins School of Theology Journal* 14 (Winter 1961): 8–9.

[12]The eleventh Article of Religion, for example, states, "We are accounted righteous before God, only for the merit of our Lord and Saviour Jesus Christ by Faith, and not for our own works or deservings. Wherefore, that we are justified by Faith only, is a most wholesome Doctrine, and very full of comfort, as more largely is expressed in the Homily of Justification." Cf. Philip Schaff, ed., *The Creeds of Christendom*, 3 vols. (Grand Rapids: Baker Book House), 3:494.

[13]Outler, "Re-Appraisal," p. 8.

[14]Jackson, *Works*, 10:403.

[15]Outler, *Works*, 1:456. (*The Lord Our Righteousness*)

[16]Jackson, *Works*, 8:111. (Emphasis mine)

[17]Frank Baker, ed., *The Works of John Wesley*, 34 vols. (New York: Oxford University Press, 1982), 25:541–42.

[18]Curnock, *Journal*, 1:424.

[19]Ibid., 1:471.

[20]Ibid. For further references to this "new" teaching, see Curnock, *Journal*, 1:457 and 1:458.

[21]Observe that after the Fetter Lane debacle Wesley was loathe to acknowledge any Moravian influence at all by maintaining that what he learned of the doctrine of justification was culled from the pages of the NT and the Anglican Homilies. Cf. John Telford, ed., *The Letters of John Wesley, A.M.*, 8 vols. (London: The Epworth Press, 1931), 4:173–74.

[22]Outler, *Works*, 1:119. (*Salvation by Faith*)

[23]Ibid.

[24]Ibid.

[25]Ibid., p. 120.

[26]Ibid.

[27]Ibid.

[28]Curnock, *Journal*, 1:471.

[29]Outler, *Works*, 1:120. (*Salvation by Faith*)

[30]Ibid., p. 121.

[31]Ibid.

[32]Ibid. (*Salvation by Faith*) For similar descriptions of this kind of faith see *Justification by Faith*, 1:193 ff., and *The Scripture Way of Salvation*, 2:160ff.

[33]Curnock, *Journal*, 1:460–80.

[34]Outler, *Works*, 2:16. (*The Original, Nature, Properties, and Use of the Law*)

[35]Ibid., 1:126–27. (*Salvation by Faith*)

[36]Ibid.

[37]Ibid., p. 127.

[38]Schaff, *Creeds*, 3:494. See also Outler's note number ninety for further references, *Works*, 1:127. (*Salvation by Faith*)

[39]Ibid., p. 128.

[40] Ibid.

[41] Ibid., p. 129.

[42] Telford, *Letters,* 4:298.

[43] Ibid. 8:178-79.

[44] Jackson, *Works,* 8:111. (Emphasis mine)

[45] Albert C. Outler, *Theology in the Wesleyan Spirit* (Nashville: Discipleship Resources, 1975), p. 53. Note that Outler's understanding of the Aldersgate experience is only one hypothesis—which is not without its own agenda, presuppositions, and problems—among many others which attempt to explain the primary evidence.

[46] Outler, *Works,* 1:186. (*Justification by Faith*)

[47] Ibid., 1:431-32. (*The Great Privilege of Those That Are Born of God*)

[48] Ibid., p. 188. (*Justification by Faith*)

[49] Ibid.

[50] Ibid., p. 189. (*Justification by Faith*) Cf. Leon Morris, *The Apostolic Preaching of the Cross* (Grand Rapids: Eerdmans Publishing Co., 1955), pp. 125ff. for an excellent treatment of the term "propitiation."

[51] Ibid., p. 188.

[52] Ibid., p. 454. (*The Lord Our Righteousness*)

[53] Ibid.

[54] Ibid., p. 455.

[55] Ibid.

[56] Ibid., p. 460. Notice that Wesley denies that the Church of Rome, William Law, and many of the Quakers, Anabaptists, and Anglicans had a proper understanding of this doctrine.

[57] Ibid., p. 462.

[58] Ibid., p. 458.

[59] Pelikan, *Luther's Works,* 26:231.

[60] McNeill, *Institutes,* 1:726-27.

[61] Outler, "Re-Appraisal," p. 8.

[62] Albert C. Outler, ed., *John Wesley* (New York: Oxford University Press, 1964), p. 52.

[63] J. Ernest Rattenbury, *The Conversion of the Wesleys* (London: The Epworth Press, 1938), p. 21.

[64] Curnock, *Journal,* 1:480.

[65] Baker, *Works,* 25:575.

[66] Curnock, *Journal,* 2:125.

[67] Baker, *Works,* 26:183.

[68] Curnock, *Journal,* 2:354.

[69] Telford, *Letters,* 2:175ff.

[70] Ibid., p. 264.

[71] Ibid., 4:298.

[72] Ibid., p. 295.

[73] Outler, *Works,* 1:456.

[74] Jackson, *Works*, 10:388.

[75] Curnock, *Journal*, 6:209.

[76] For further evidence of this chronology see Telford, *Letters*, 258–59; 6:331; and Jackson, *Works*, 7:317; 10:403.

[77] Outler, *Wesley*, p. 14.

[78] Ibid.

[79] Ibid., p. 51.

[80] Ibid. (Bracketed material mine)

[81] Ibid., p. 51–53.

[82] Outler, "Re-Appraisal," p. 8.

[83] Curnock, *Journal*, 1:424. (Emphasis mine)

[84] Ibid., 2:30.

[85] Outler, *Wesley*, p. 51.

[86] Telford, *Letters*, 5:16. The bracketed material was written in shorthand which meant that it was for Charles' eyes only.

[87] Cf. Wesley's sermon, *The Spirit of Bondage and of Adoption* in Outler, *Works*, 1:248–66.

[88] Ibid., 1:442.

[89] Outler, "Re-Appraisal," pp. 8–9.

[90] Outler, *Wesley*, p. 14.

[91] Curnock, *Journal*, 1:475–76.

[92] Albert C. Outler, "Beyond Pietism: Aldersgate in Context," *Motive*, Vol. 23, No. 8 (May 1963), p. 13.

[93] Ibid., p. 477.

[94] Telford, *Letters*, 3:302.

[95] Curnock, *Journal*, 1:109. For further references to Wesley's lack of spiritual power, see 1:138, 140, 246, 413, 415, 417, 418, 419, 420, and 422.

[96] Ibid., p. 422, and for a second reference see p. 418. At times the cruciality of Aldersgate is repudiated in light of the distinction that Wesley drew between the faith of a servant and the faith of a son. But if anything, such a distinction not only does not minimize the importance of Aldersgate but actually supports it. For while it is certainly true that Wesley referred to his own early experience prior to May 1738 in terms of the former faith, that is, as the faith of a servant, notice that the prerogatives of the latter are exercised only by those born of God. That this analysis is correct is substantiated in Wesley's sermon *The Discoveries of Faith* by his discussion of the faith of a servant in terms of "the spirit of bondage unto fear," (Jackson, *Works*, 7:236. Also compare with Wesley's commentary on Romans chapter seven.) and the faith of a son in terms of the "spirit of childlike love" (Ibid). That the faith of a servant—and the spirit of bondage for that matter—represents a measure of faith is granted, but that it is indicative of regeneration is not. Listen to Wesley: "Exhort him to press on, by all possible means, till he passes 'from faith to faith'; from the faith of a servant to the faith of a son; from the spirit of bondage unto fear, to the

spirit of childlike love: He will then have 'Christ revealed in his heart' "
(Ibid).

[97]This position as well is not without its problems. This was
pointed out to me by Dr. Ted Campbell who referred me to the part of
the 24 May entry which reads, "I believe, till I was about ten years old I
had not sinned away that 'washing of the Holy Ghost' which was given
me in baptism. . . ." (1:465) Indeed, there is a sense in which Wesley
does associate regeneration with baptism in a sacramental way, but he
also understands the new birth in an "evangelical" way as the time
when the believer experiences freedom from the guilt and power of sin.
Cf. Ole E. Borgen, *John Wesley on the Sacraments* (Grand Rapids:
Zondervan/Francis Asbury Press, 1972), pp. 121–182.

[98]Outler, "Beyond Pietism," p. 12.

[99]Curnock, *Journal*, 1:479–80.

IV

THE NEW BIRTH
AND ASSURANCE

Two of the fundamental doctrines of Christianity, according to Wesley, are justification and the new birth. Chronologically speaking, neither of these doctrines is realized before the other in the life of the believer: that is, at the same time that justification takes place, the new birth, or what Wesley sometimes refers to as initial sanctification, occurs as well. In fact, the new birth for Wesley is "the gate" to the whole process of sanctification; it is the beginning of the development of the life of God in the soul.[1]

Now although Wesley does not make a temporal distinction between these fundamental doctrines he does make a logical one. In his sermon "The New Birth," for example, he writes, "In order of thinking, as it is termed, justification precedes the new birth. We first conceive his wrath to be turned away, and then his Spirit to work in our hearts."[2] Beyond this, Wesley draws attention to the different natures of these doctrines by noting that "justification implies only a relative, the new birth a real, change. God in justifying us does something *for* us: in begetting us again he does the work *in* us."[3] Put another way, justification changes the outward relation to God so that sinners are now restored to the divine favor; they are freed from the power of guilt. Regeneration, on the other hand, changes the inward nature of people so that they are initially made holy; they are freed from the power of sin.

Both of these liberties just enumerated—freedom from the guilt and the power of sin—are indispensable aspects of what Wesley means by the term salvation. Again, neither ingredient can stand alone nor is one to be emphasized to the detriment of the other. And it is precisely on this score, concerning the relation of these two fundamental doctrines of Christianity, that Wesley faults other church traditions for their largely unbalanced approach. He observes:

> Many who have spoken and written admirably well concerning justification had no clear conception, nay, were totally ignorant, of the doctrine of sanctification. Who has wrote more ably than Martin Luther on justification by faith alone? And who was more ignorant of the doctrine of sanctification, or more confused in his conceptions of it? . . . On the other hand, how many writers of the Romish Church (as Francis Sales and Juan de Castaniza in particular) have wrote strongly and scripturally on sanctification; who nevertheless were entirely unacquainted with the nature of justification.[4]

In a note that some might contend smacks of triumphalism, Wesley adds, "It has pleased God to give the Methodists a full and clear knowledge of each, and the wide difference between them."[5]

The genius of Wesley's theology, therefore, consists in his attentiveness not only to the issues of justification and forgiveness, like the Reformers, but to those which concerned the "Catholic" tradition as well, such as the new birth and holiness. For Wesley, these diverse doctrines are drawn in relation to one another through vital faith which is the common element, the nexus, between them. Indeed, the forgiveness of sins is received and the life of God is established in the soul only by this means. Faith's function, then, is not singular but at least two-fold in Wesley's theology, and that both operations are absolutely necessary to the Christian life is evidenced by his precautionary remark: "We esteem no faith but that 'which worketh by love'; and that we are not 'saved by faith' unless so far as we are delivered from the power as well as the guilt of sin."[6]

THE NEW BIRTH

Having distinguished the doctrine of justification from regeneration in a cursory fashion, it is now appropriate to explore the latter doctrine in some detail. An important question which first comes to mind, though it is not often asked, is why have a doctrine of the new birth at all. In other words, why is justification by faith, and the forgiveness associated with it, not sufficient to rectify the problems of the sinner? Almost as if in response to these very queries, Wesley maintains in his sermon *The New Birth,* produced in 1760, that the sinner's need is far greater than the reception of forgiveness, since there is a life yet to be lived. If one's nature, for instance, is not transformed, how can the Christian life be lived with any degree of satisfaction? For this, a further work is needed.

Another way that Wesley expresses the need for regeneration is to draw a tight association between this doctrine and that of original sin. In his mind, each is to be interpreted in light of the other. And to further this end, Wesley reviews the Genesis accounts afresh. Originally, God created humanity in His own image and likeness: in the natural, political and moral image of the Most High.[7] In this pristine state, Wesley argues, humanity exercised its spiritual powers in the love of God and neighbor, sincerely and purely. Humanity was created "able to stand, and yet liable to fall."[8] But fall it did. Where there was once fellowship with God, now there was separation. Servile fear replaced humanity's confidence; people became unhappy precisely because they were unholy. And worst of all, humanity died to the life of God, and was now steeped in "pride, self-will, the very image of the devil, and [it fell] into sensual appetites and desires, the image of the beasts that perish."[9] Therefore, the foundation of the new birth is, in the words of Wesley, "the entire corruption of our nature."[10] And as has already been indicated in chapter one, failure to comprehend original sin properly often results in a weak doctrine of regeneration. But for Wesley, each doctrine is to be interpreted in light of the other with the result that the need for a moral and spiritual renovation is clear. The new birth is necessary in order to create both happiness and holiness in the life of the believer. Forgiveness is not enough.

Having established that one must be born again, Wesley then entertains inquiries concerning the nature of this renewal. Admittedly, this is a difficult subject even for Wesley, if simply because of the fact that flesh and blood human beings have a rather difficult time understanding things of a spiritual nature. But Wesley, ever mindful of the spiritual level of his hearers, helps them along in his sermons by drawing an analogy between what is familiar and what is unfamiliar, between the natural realm and the spiritual realm. Along these lines, he likens the new birth to natural birth and proceeds accordingly.

Consider a child in its mother's womb, Wesley reasons, it does not feel; it hears very little; it sees not at all. From a certain perspective, it has no senses: "All these avenues of the soul are hitherto quite shut up."[11] But such is also the case with those persons who are not yet born of God. Like unborn children, their spiritual senses are largely dormant. Their vision is blurred, "a thick impenetrable veil lies upon them."[12] They have ears, but they do not hear. They have little knowledge of God or communion with Him; spiritual concerns and a consideration of eternity baffles them.[13] Moreover, though these people are alive, yet in another more important sense they are dead, dead to God and to the power of His sanctifying and regenerating grace. They are, according to Wesley, "dead Christians."[14]

Continuing the analogy, what of the child when it is thrust forth from its mother's womb? It is then, Wesley reckons, that it begins to exist in quite a different manner. It now feels the air which surrounds it; its eyes are opened to see the light of this world; its ears hear the sounds that before it only dimly perceived. Every sense is employed in relation to its proper object. Even so is it with those who are born of God. The children of God now see the glorious love of God manifested in Jesus Christ. They hear the inward voice of God saying, "Be of good cheer, thy sins are forgiven thee."[15] They feel the mighty working of the Holy Spirit in their hearts, and are conscious of a "peace which passeth all understanding."[16] All their spiritual senses are awake, with the result that they increase daily in the knowledge of God and His love. Of this magnificent change Wesley writes:

> From hence it manifestly appears what is the nature of the new birth. It is that great change which God works in the soul when he brings it into life: when he raises it from the death of sin to the life of righteousness. It is the change wrought in the whole soul by the almighty Spirit of God when it is "created anew in Christ Jesus," when it is "renewed after the image of God, in righteousness and true holiness". . . .[17]

Two additional points need to be made. First, the spiritual senses, Wesley implies, are activated and are directed to their proper objects through faith. In the last chapter, it will be recalled, faith was defined mainly, though not exclusively, in terms of both an intellectual assent and a hearty trust in God. But in this present context, in terms of spiritual perception, faith is understood in a much more general fashion, as a "divine, supernatural evidence or conviction of things not seen, not discoverable by our bodily senses. . . ."[18] Faith, therefore, is the principal organ for spiritual knowledge and discernment in the well-developed Christian life; it is the major channel through which the enabling graces of God are received. In addition, it is faith which is behind all of the many spiritual senses already discussed: the seeing eye, the hearing ear, and the feeling heart. Understood in this fashion, faith becomes, for all practical purposes, a sixth sense for Wesley, exercised in both justification and the new birth where it not only receives the forgiveness of God, but His power and grace as well.

Second, Wesley milks the analogy between natural and spiritual birth further to describe the nature of the temporal elements involved. He explains that a child is born of woman "in a moment, or at least in a very short time."[19] After this, the child continues to grow until it reaches maturity. In the same way, Wesley argues, "a child is born of God in a short time, if not in a moment. But it is by slow degrees that he afterward grows up to the measure of the full 'stature of Christ.' "[20] The relation, then, which holds between natural birth and maturation is similar to the relation between the new birth and sanctification. In other words, Wesley is attentive to the crisis of the new birth *and* the process of sanctification; both aspects are acknowledged. Furthermore, it appears that Wesley takes great pains to warn his hearers of the false and damaging notion that the new birth is something which occurs as a matter of course in the spiritual life, as if one could simply grow into it.

Moreover, in his sermon *The Witness of the Spirit: Discourse One*, Wesley cautions against following the path of the presumptuous, those who have never questioned or doubted their Christian status: "But what knoweth he concerning whom we now speak of any such change as this? He is altogether unacquainted with this whole matter. This is a language which he does not understand. He tells you he always was a Christian. He knows no time when he had need of such a change."[21] In other words, for the leader of the British revival, the process of salvation is punctuated by crises that are deep not superficial, thorough not partial, and serious not insignificant. To deny, therefore, either the element of crisis in the fear of fanaticism or process in the fear of dead orthodoxy is to fail to appreciate the balance and the eminent sensibility of Wesley's position.

The Marks of the New Birth

In his sermon, *The Marks of the New Birth,* preached in 1739 at the very beginning of the revival, Wesley once again explores the nature of the new birth, but this time in terms of the marks or graces associated with it: namely, faith, hope, and love. Concerning faith, the first characteristic, Wesley reiterates the by-now-familiar themes that faith is not only an assent to divine truth, but also a confidence in the mercy of God through Jesus Christ. A new emphasis, however, emerges in his remarks that a fruit of the faith through which one is born again, and which cannot be separated from it, is power over sin, "power over outward sin of every kind; over every evil word and work . . . This fruit of faith St. Paul has largely described in the sixth chapter of his Epistle to the Romans."[22]

Admittedly, this last issue of freedom from the power of sin is often misunderstood even within Methodism, mainly because people are not willing to take the time to consider, first of all, what Wesley means by sin, properly speaking, and, second, what a rigorous and lofty view of the normal Christian life Wesley actually paints. Concerning the first issue, and in answer to the question in what sense does one who is born of God not commit sin, Wesley writes:

> By "sin" I here understand outward sin, according to the plain, common acceptation [sic] of the word: an actual, voluntary "transgression of the law"; of the revealed, written law of God; of any commandment of God acknowledged to be such at the time that it is transgressed. But "whosoever is born of God," . . . not only "doth not," but "cannot" thus "commit sin."[23]

Notice that Wesley's definition of sin incorporates a volitional component; there must be willful consent for sin to occur. All mistakes and errors, therefore, though they may be transgressions of the law of God, are not sins, properly speaking, if they lack the force of the will. Notice also that Wesley defines sin in terms of the revealed and written law of

God. This fact should prove troubling to those scholars who maintain that Wesley's essential understanding of sin is expressed mainly in relational terms, not legal ones.[24] However, it is more to the point to argue that both terms are factored into Wesley's conception.

With respect to the second issue, that Wesley had a rigorous and lofty conception of the normal Christian life, it should be pointed out that he was well aware of the evasion—offered even in his own day—that a child of God is not one who does not commit sin, but one who does not commit it *habitually*. To this, he replies, "But some men will say, 'True; whosoever is born of God doth not commit sin *habitually*'. *Habitually!* Whence is that? I read it not. It is not written in the Book. God plainly saith, he 'doth not commit sin'. And thou addest, 'habitually'!"[25]

By the exclusion of the word "habitually" from this context, Wesley believes he is safeguarding one of the precious promises of the gospel, that so long as the saints abide in the love of God and continue to believe, they will not sin. In other words, regenerating faith and sin are mutually exclusive in Wesley's thought; when the one appears the other vanishes. In fact, Wesley details the slow and subtle process of the loss of faith and a descent into sin—what some might call a reversal of the *ordo salutis*—in his sermon, *The Great Privilege of Those That Are Born of God*.[26] Nevertheless, his emphasis is elsewhere; not on human sin and weakness, but on the sufficiency of God's grace. The optimism of grace, therefore, not the pessimism of nature, is the chord struck here.

If, on the other hand, the word "habitually" is retained, Wesley fears it will result in a definition of a Christian in terms of sin, that somehow or other sin will be considered a normal and expected part of the Christian life. To this, however, he replies with a resounding No! Committing sin is not normal in Christian experience; it is the grave exception rather than the rule. And Wesley holds to this standard of teaching in his sermons because he believes it to be scriptural. In fact, on this particular subject, his homilies are replete with numerous citations from the writings of both Paul and John indicating that this doctrine reflects not his own idiosyncrasies but the Bible itself.

Does Wesley's doctrine of sin, then, mean that those who are born of God can never sin again? Moreover, does the evidence of sin subsequent to the new birth indicate that one was never truly born of God? To these questions, also, Wesley replies with a resounding No! He writes:

> It is plain, in fact, that those whom we cannot deny to have been truly 'born of God' nevertheless not only could but did commit sin, even gross, outward sin. They did transgress the plain, known laws of God, speaking or acting what they know he had forbidden. . . . I answer, what has been long observed is this: so long as 'he that is born of God keepeth himself' (which he is able to do by the grace of God) 'the wicked one toucheth him not.' But if he keepeth not himself, if he abide not in the faith, he may commit sin even as another man.[27]

Such language highlights not only the moment by moment dependence of the believer on God, but also the availability of divine life-sustaining grace to the believer. Therefore, a Christian not only can but should be free from the power of sin. Nevertheless, the Christian can fall through a loss of faith and sin like any other person. Wesley holds both these ideas together.

Yet another way that this first mark of the new birth—that faith delivers from the power of sin—can be misunderstood is to hold a lower estimate of regeneration than Wesley does, and to consider the powers, graces, and privileges delineated above as descriptive not of the new birth but of Christian perfection. To avoid this error, one must note the distinction that Wesley makes in terms of freedom from sin as it relates to the new birth and as it relates to entire sanctification. In the former instance, one is free from the guilt and power of sin; in the latter, one is free from the *being* of sin, even the carnal nature.[28] The difference is important.

From the issue of faith, Wesley proceeds to consider the second mark of the new birth which is hope. But since this aspect is strongly associated with the doctrine of assurance, both in terms of the Spirit's witness and the witness of our own spirit (conscience), it will be treated in detail under a separate heading below. However, the third mark of the new birth, and the greatest of all, is love. For believers, the love of God is shed abroad in their hearts by the Holy Spirit. They are enabled through grace to call upon God as their protector and to cry in a familial and intimate way, "Abba Father." God is, in the words of Wesley, "the joy of their heart, their shield, and their exceeding great reward."[29] And an immediate and necessary fruit of this divine love incarnate in the believer is the love of neighbor, "of every soul which God hath made; not excepting our enemies . . . a love whereby we love every man *as ourselves*—as we love our own souls."[30]

Though Wesley places great emphasis on the relationship between God and humanity as seen in the context of personal and mutual love, it is interesting to note that he still insists on a role for the moral law as a guide and mirror of that relationship; it has not dropped out. Thus, one of the ways of conceiving the love of God and neighbor, Wesley affirms, so that it does not result in mere sentimentality, is in terms of the moral law which is an "incorruptible picture of the high and holy One that inhabiteth eternity." [31] He observes:

> This is the sign or proof of the love of God, of our keeping the first and great commandment—to keep the rest of his commandments. For true love, if it be once shed abroad in our heart, will constrain us so to do; since whosoever loves God with all his heart cannot but serve him with all his strength.[32]

By way of summary, then, the scriptural marks of the new birth include faith which delivers from the power of sin, hope which is sustained by the joint witness of God's Spirit and our own that we are indeed His children, and the love of God which fills the believer with the joy of the Holy Spirit and which reaches out, in an unselfish way, to embrace the neighbor.

Baptism and the New Birth

In his Journal on 24 May 1738, Wesley wrote, "I believe, till I was about ten years old I had not sinned away that 'washing of the Holy Ghost' which was given me in baptism."[33] Now if the phrase "washing of the Holy Ghost" is identified with the graces of regeneration, a likely inference, then it reveals that even after his evangelical conversion, Wesley still retained a sacramental view of the new birth. But elsewhere he specifically wrote that baptism is not the new birth.[34] How are these two apparently contradictory statements to be reconciled, if at all?

It should first of all be observed that Wesley viewed the

sacrament of baptism as a sign, an external work, which points to the thing signified, an internal work.[35] With this distinction in hand, Wesley was able to maintain that though the sign of water cleansing is often accompanied by the thing signified, the new birth, it is not always so. Where the identification of these items is closest, however, if not exact, is in terms of infant baptism, for it seems that Wesley never renounced the teaching of the Anglican Church which moved along these lines. So when Wesley asserted that the new birth does not always accompany baptism, he immediately added, "I do not now speak with regard to infants: it is certain, our Church supposes that all who are baptized in their infancy are at the same time born again."[36]

But, on the other hand, Wesley was also familiar with numerous instances of those who had been baptized in either infancy or in their later years who yet had none of the marks of the new birth: "How many are the baptized gluttons and drunkards, the baptized liars and common swearers, the baptized railers and evil-speakers, the baptized whoremongers, thieves, extortioners?"[37] he asked. "What think you? Are these now the children of God?"[38] The implication is clear. Therefore, Wesley the itinerant preacher and revivalist was not content simply with a sacramental view of the new birth, for an evangelical one emerges as well. Those born of God should bear the proper fruit. And if these evidences are lacking, then they must be called to repentance and renewal, despite the fact that baptism has already occurred.

ASSURANCE

When Wesley recounted the Aldersgate experience in his Journal in 1738, he wrote, among other things, "an assurance was given me that He had taken away *my* sins, even *mine,* and saved *me* from the law of sin and death."[39] Observe that in this context assurance has two focal points. It pertains not only to a sense of forgiveness, but also to freedom from the law of sin and death. That is, assurance encompasses both justification and the new birth, freedom from the guilt *and* the power of sin. To be sure, the discussion of Wesley's doctrine of assurance, as reflected in his sermons, has been reserved precisely until now to highlight this dual perspective. Assurance does not simply relate to the issues of justification and forgiveness. As Wesley put it, "We must be holy of heart and holy in life before we can be conscious that we are so."[40] Both referents are necessary.

As the principal objects to which assurance refers are two, the subjects which engender this sense of peace, joy and well-being are also of two kinds: namely, the witness of our own spirit and the witness of God's Spirit. In fact, so interested was Wesley in this topic—since he saw it as one of the privileges of the children of God—he wrote at least three sermons directly pertaining to it.

In an important homily on this subject, *The Witness of the Spirit Discourse One,* written in 1746, Wesley views the first witness, that of our own spirit, as an indirect one in the sense that an inference has to be made concerning several evidences in order for this witness to be confirmed. Some of the evidence which Wesley consults are all those marks of the new birth such as faith, hope, and love which have already been noted above. Beyond this, Wesley points to obedience to the commandments of God as a sign, though certainly not as a cause, of a favored state with God. These rational evidences, and others, when taken together, lead to the conclusion that one is a child of God. In fact, Wesley often employs syllogisms in these sermons to display how the proper deduction is made, one of which is the following:

> First, "As many as are led by the Spirit of God" into all holy tempers and actions, "they are the sons of God" (for which he has the infallible assurance of Holy Writ); secondly, I am thus "led by the Spirit of God"—he will easily conclude, "Therefore I am a 'son of God.'"[41]

But the evidence to which Wesley most often refers with respect to the witness of our own spirit comes from conscience. This faculty, Wesley teaches, involves much more than mere consciousness, for not only does it bring to mind the past, but it also exercises judgment upon it. In one sense, this power seems to be a natural one because it is manifested in all human beings in their determinations of right and wrong. However, Wesley insists that its origin is from God who implants it in every human being; its source, therefore, is not from nature but from grace. That Wesley considers conscience an important aspect of prevenient grace is substantiated by his following remarks:

For though in one sense [conscience] may be termed "natural," because it is found in all men, yet properly speaking it is not *natural*; but a supernatural gift of God, above all his natural endowments. No, it is not nature but the Son of God that is "the true light, which enlighteneth every man which cometh into the world."[42]

Moreover, according to Wesley, the rule or standard which conscience employs in the moral and spiritual life is for non-Christians "the law written in their hearts,"[43] and for Christians "the Word of God, the writings of the Old and New Testament."[44] In good Protestant fashion, Wesley assigns reason an important though secondary role with respect to moral authority; the highest place, of course, is given to Scripture. "This is a lantern unto a Christian's feet," Wesley writes, "and a light in all his paths. This alone he receives as his rule of right or wrong, of whatever is really good or evil."[45]

A good conscience, a faculty properly ordered, emerges when a number of items are brought into play. There must first of all be a proper understanding of the Word of God, the principal standard for the Christian, "for it is impossible we should walk by a rule if we do not know what it means."[46] Secondly, true knowledge of ourselves, of our hearts and lives is required; that is, a good conscience must necessarily exclude self-deception and be accurately informed concerning one's true moral state. Furthermore, there must exist an essential agreement between our lives, on the one hand, and the rule of Scripture on the other. And it is precisely this habitual perception of harmony between norm and life which Wesley deems a "good conscience."[47]

As important as the witness of our own spirit is in Wesley's doctrine of assurance, it does not constitute the entirety of what he means by this doctrine. If this witness, for example, were the only one taken into account, there would then be a risk of formalism or even legalism as one attempted to infer one's Christian status from works or rational evidences. But Wesley does not leave it at this, and goes on to argue that there is a witness over and above all these rational evidences just cited. He is referring, of course, to the witness of God's Spirit which is the privilege—though many are ignorant of it—of all who believe.

This witness of God's Spirit, unlike the witness of our own, is immediate and direct. It is immediate in the sense that no time is needed for this witness; it comes neither at the end of a rational process nor as the result of an inference. It is direct in the sense that the Holy Spirit Himself bears witness that one is a child of God. Obedience to the commandments, for example, may point to one's holiness, but when the Holy Spirit who is the source of all holiness bears witness, this is primary testimony indeed! In addition, the direct witness of the Spirit can be distinguished from the fruit of the Spirit, an inferential witness, when it is realized that the former is in a real sense the cause of the latter. That Wesley does, in fact, draw a relation between the two is borne out by the following:

> The testimony now under consideration is given by the Spirit of God to and with our spirit. He is the person testifying. What he testifies to us is "that we are the children of God." The immediate result of this testimony is the "fruit of the Spirit"; namely, "love, joy, peace; longsuffering, gentleness, goodness." And without these the testimony itself cannot continue.[48]

But notice in the material just offered that Wesley indicates a dialectical relationship between the two kinds of witness. Without doubt, the result of the Holy Spirit's witness is the fruit of the Spirit, but the former witness cannot continue if the latter is lacking: that is, there cannot be any real testimony of the Spirit without the fruit of the Spirit. Both testimonies, then, are necessary ingredients for Wesley's doctrine of assurance. No one witness can stand alone.

Now the objects of the Spirit's witness—of which it gives testimony—are two and correspond to the major referents of the doctrine of assurance. Wesley explains: "The testimony of the Spirit is an inward impression on the soul, whereby the Spirit of God directly 'witnesses to my spirit that I am a child of God'; that Jesus Christ hath loved me, and given himself for me; that all my sins are blotted out, and I, even I, am reconciled to God."[49]

But if the witness of our own spirit has the same two objects, why is there a need for the additional witness of the Spirit, and why does Wesley emphasize it so in his sermons, despite numerous objections? First, the indirect witness may be under a cloud through heaviness or through the onslaught of severe temptations, and yet the direct witness may shine clearly all the while.[50] In other words, the immediate witness of the

Spirit is not subject to the whims of human emotions, tempers, and faulty reasoning, and therefore is to be valued. Second, Wesley contends that whoever denies the existence of the direct witness denies justification by faith as well.[51] In other words, without the witness of the Spirit one is left with evidences, inferences, works, etc.—all of which have the potential and danger of resulting in self-justification. To safeguard against this error, to protect the graciousness of *sola fide,* the witness of God's Holy Spirit is required. Third, Wesley stresses the direct witness because he believes it is confirmed by the Word of God (Rom. 8:16) and by Christian experience. Why, then, let go of such an important witness?

By way of summary, then, Wesley in his sermons on Christian assurance is attempting to avoid two extremes. On the one hand is the ever-present danger of "enthusiasm" or fanaticism which can occur when believers rest solely on the witness of the Spirit to the neglect of the fruit of the Spirit and rational evidence. This presumption can be avoided, however, through close attention to the elements which compose the indirect witness such as the marks of the new birth, the fruit of the Spirit, obedience to the commandments, and appeal to Scripture as a norm and guide. And so to this first group, the enthusiasts, Wesley warns, "Let none ever presume to rest in any supposed testimony of the Spirit which is separate from the fruit of it."[52]

On the other hand, Wesley was familiar, in his enlightened age, with the repudiation of the direct witness of the Spirit fostered in some degree by fear of the excesses of the first group, the fanatics. Here, the fruit of the Spirit and the other indirect evidence are emphasized and are deemed the entirety of what constitutes assurance. All else is considered rank "enthusiasm." The danger of this position, as noted earlier, is in terms of the specter of formalism, legalism, and self-justification. There simply must be a witness other than the self to create the kind of peace and assurance which will sustain the Christian life. And so to this second group, the rationalists, Wesley issues a warning, "Let none rest in any supposed fruit of the Spirit without the witness. There may be foretastes of joy, of peace, of love—and those not delusive, but really from God."[53]

It should be apparent by now that Wesley's doctrine of assurance is a balanced one. It was forged in the heat of controversy and criticism; it did not emerge simply through reading and study.[54] Characteristic of his pastoral style, Wesley's sermons were directed to the needs of both enthusiasts and rationalists; he was as comfortable directing his comments to Bishop Lavington, a rationalist, as he was to the most rank enthusiast. Neither had a corner on the truth, yet each had an important, though often exaggerated, contribution to make. And so Wesley endeavored through the course of the years to get each group to see a larger picture than each had imagined. A well-informed balance was, therefore, his constant aim, and attentiveness to those who disagreed with him was his ever-present goal. Such factors as these are typical of Wesley's basic theological posture and are part of the rich legacy that he has left to his heirs.

NOTES

[1] Outler, *Works,* 3:506. (*On God's Vineyard*)
[2] Ibid., 2:187. (*The New Birth*)
[3] Ibid., 1:431–32. (*The Great Privilege of Those That Are Born of God*)
[4] Ibid., 3:505–06. (*On God's Vineyard*)
[5] Ibid.
[6] Ibid., 1:559–60. (*Sermon on the Mount, V*+p)
[7] Ibid., 2:188. (*The New Birth*)
[8] Ibid., p. 189.
[9] Ibid., pp. 189–90. (Bracketed material mine)
[10] Ibid., p. 190.
[11] Ibid., 1:433. (*The Great Privilege of Those That Are Born of God*) See also 2:192ff. (*The New Birth*) for a further delineation of the natural and spiritual senses.
[12] Ibid., 2:192. (*The New Birth*) I have taken the liberty here to join together two similar strains in Wesley's thought that are reflected in separate sermons. *The Great Privilege of Those That Are Born of God* employs the imagery of a child in its mother's womb, and this state has been compared to that of the "natural man" in the sermon *The New Birth*. Compare 1:433ff. with 2:192ff.
[13] Ibid.
[14] Ibid.
[15] Ibid. See also *The Spirit of Bondage and of Adoption* for a developmental description of the change which takes place in the new birth. 1:263.
[16] Ibid., 2:192–93.
[17] Ibid., pp. 193–94.
[18] Ibid., 1:194. (*Justification by Faith*) There is no intention to deny the intuitive function of faith with respect to justification. No doubt,

the forgiveness of God is discerned in the same manner as the righteousness and holiness or any other attribute of God. Nevertheless, since it is in his discussion of the new birth that Wesley most clearly explores the spiritual senses, and the faith which they reflect, a discussion of the intuitive nature of faith was left until this point.

[19] Ibid., 2:198. (*The New Birth*)

[20] Ibid.

[21] Ibid., 1:279. (*The Witness of the Spirit, Discourse One*) But keep in mind that Wesley was no date-setter. One might not know the exact time when the new birth occurred, but one should know *that* it occurred.

[22] Ibid., 1:419. (*The Marks of the New Birth*)

[23] Ibid., 1:436. (*The Great Privilege of Those That Are Born of God*)

[24] Colin Williams sees "great dangers" in defining sin in terms of a voluntary transgression of a known law of God. He much prefers to view sin in relational terms, as a "conscious separation from Christ." Moreover, it appears that the moral law as a norm or standard simply drops out in Williams' assessment of Wesley's doctrine of Christian perfection. But Wesley stressed the continual importance of the law at every stage of the Christian walk. The law leads to Christ and Christ leads back to the law, neither movement is repudiated. Cf. *The Law Established by Faith Discourse I & II.* Outler, *Works*, 2:20–43. See also Colin Williams, *John Wesley's Theology Today* (Nashville: Abingdon Press, 1960), pp. 178–81.

[25] Outler, *Works*, 1:420. (*The Marks of the New Birth*)

[26] Ibid., 1:439ff. (*The Great Privilege of Those That Are Born of God*)

[27] Ibid., 1:436, 438. (*The Great Privilege of Those That Are Born of God*) In the case of willful sin after the new birth, one does not again have to be born again but instead one must be restored to the high grace from which one has fallen.

[28] See the sermons *On Sin in Believers,* and *The Repentance of Believers,* 1:314ff., and 1:335ff.

[29] Ibid., 1:425. (*The Marks of the New Birth*)

[30] Ibid., p. 426.

[31] Ibid., 2:9. (*The Original, Nature, Properties, and Use of the Law*)

[32] Ibid., 1:427. (*The Marks of the New Birth*)

[33] Curnock, *Journal*, 1:465.

[34] Outler, *Works*, 2:196. (*The New Birth*)

[35] Ibid. For an extensive treatment of the relation between the new birth and baptism in Wesley's thought see Ole E. Borgen, *John Wesley on the Sacraments* (Grand Rapids: Zondervan/Francis Asbury Press, 1972), pp. 121–82.

[36] Ibid., p. 197.

[37] Ibid., 1:429. (*The Marks of the New Birth*)

[38] Ibid.

[39] Curnock, *Journal*, 1:476.

[40] Outler, *Works,* 1:274. (*The Witness of the Spirit, Discourse I*)
[41] Ibid., pp. 271–72.
[42] Ibid., 3:482. (*On Conscience*)
[43] Ibid., 1:302. (*The Witness of Our Own Spirit*)
[44] Ibid.
[45] Ibid., p. 303.
[46] Ibid., pp. 303–4.
[47] Ibid., p. 304.
[48] Ibid., 1:285. (*The Witness of the Spirit, Discourse II*)
[49] Ibid., p. 274. (*The Witness of the Spirit, Discourse I*)
[50] Ibid., p. 294. (*The Witness of the Spirit, Discourse II*)
[51] Ibid., p. 292.
[52] Ibid., p. 297.
[53] Ibid., p. 298.
[54] Dr. Lavington, the Bishop of Exeter, had assailed Wesley with the most acute invective; he accused Wesley, among other things, of enthusiasm, fanaticism, and of a "most abominable communion in its most corrupt ages." Cf. Telford, *Letters,* 3:259.

V

THE NATURE OF THE
CHRISTIAN LIFE:
Personal and Social Ethics

GRACE

One of the areas of Wesley's theology which is continually misunderstood, by Methodist and non-Methodist alike, is his doctrine of grace. Yet if there is any one strain of thought which holds his sermons and preached theology together, it is this. One possible explanation for failure to grasp Wesley's essential teaching in this key area is that many Protestants form their notions of grace at the feet of Calvin and Luther and then make these Reformers the standard. Subsequently, when Wesley's theology is considered, they are surprised to learn that his notion of grace is both similar and different from the continental Reformers. The remedy for such dissonance—though not to all the theological problems entailed—is to place Wesley in his proper historical setting, to realize that his thought takes its direction not from Geneva or Wittenberg but from Canterbury, from the English Reformation, and from the genius of Cranmer in particular. Indeed, Wesley's doctrine of grace, when viewed properly, emerges as one of the many fine examples of the Anglican *via media*.

As noted in Chapter 1, Wesley is most similar to the continental Reformers in his emphasis that the grace of God is unmerited, free in all to whom it is given,[1] and that it represents divine favor and approval. Put another way, God is never in our debt because of anything we have done; all our obedience is already owed, and there is nothing "extra" to offer up that could possibly obligate God. In Wesley's own words, "All the blessings which God hath bestowed upon man are of his mere grace, bounty, or favour: his free, undeserved favour, favour altogether undeserved. . ."[2] Salvation is by grace through faith. In this, at least, there is agreement.

But as important as this idea is, it does not constitute the entirety of what Wesley means by the grace of God. In fact, he draws two further important conclusions from the premise of the priority of divine action. In his sermon *On Working Out Our Own Salvation,* for example, he reasons that if it really is God who works in us, then we can work. The grace of God, therefore, creates the ability to perform what is required. But notice that even here this ability does not entail human merit, for it is God, not the believer, who is the principal agent. Yet the believer works. Wesley writes:

> Therefore inasmuch as God works in you, you are now able to work out your own salvation. Since he worketh in you of his own good pleasure, without any merit of yours, both to will and to do, it is possible for you to fulfill all righteousness. It is possible for you to "love God, because he hath first loved us."[3]

Grace, so conceived, is the dynamic power of God made available to all who believe. And Wesley cautioned the Methodists to beware of that pessimism and mock humility which "teacheth us to say, in excuse for our willful disobedience, 'Oh, I can do nothing,' and stops there, without once naming the grace of God."[4] Divine empowerment, not human ability, is the chord struck here. We can do all things through Christ who strengthens us.

The second conclusion Wesley draws from the priority of God's action is that if God works in us, then we must work. Increasing ability as the result of divine grace involves its recipients in greater responsibilities. "You must be workers together with him," Wesley contends, "otherwise he will cease working."[5] The grace of God, therefore, must either be improved or lost. There is no standing still. "Stir up the spark of grace which is now in you," Wesley admonishes, "and he will give you more grace."[6]

In light of the preceding, it is evident that Wesley conceives the divine/human relationship synergistically: that is, in terms of both divine initiative and human response. God is the source of all, to be sure, but God does not do all. Quoting Augustine, Wesley writes, " 'He that made us without ourselves, will not save us without ourselves.' "[7] Not surprisingly then, Wesley's doctrine of prevenient, convincing, and sanctifying grace all evidence this motif of synergism. God initiates, enables, and thereby creates responsibility in humans. "No man sins," Wesley observes, "because he has not grace, but because he does not use the grace which he hath."[8] Moreover, there is a real sense in Wesley's thought that as grace is increased—in other words as one progressively receives the prevenient, convincing, and saving grace of God—ability and responsibility are increased as well.

From one perspective, when the process of salvation is conceived synergistically, as in Wesley's thought, the onus appears to be upon the believer once grace is given. But Wesley did not balk at such prospect. In fact, he constantly exhorted those under his spiritual tutelage to strain, to strive, to work, and to labor in light of the rich and powerful grace of God. But notice how United Methodist theologian William Cannon inverts—and some would suggest distorts—this synergism. He writes, "The conception of human initiative and divine response is likewise descriptive of his teaching and is not alien to his theology. Why? Simply because divine initiative in bestowing common or preventing grace is taken for granted."[9]

In opposition to Cannon, it should be noted that Wesley's doctrine of grace, technically speaking, gives no support to "human initiative," in the sense of a first move apart from grace, although it can and does sustain a thorough-going synergism. For Wesley, the first movement toward salvation can be undertaken only by God. But precisely because God has acted, human *response* is possible. God's prior activity, although presupposed, must never be taken for granted.

THE MORAL LAW REMAINS

When John Wesley finally comprehended the full import of the doctrine of justification by faith on both an intellectual and experiential level, this in no way detracted from his earlier emphasis on the holy life, an emphasis that can be traced back to as early as 1725. But when he surveyed the spiritual landscape of eighteenth century England, he noticed the tendency among many Protestants to undervalue the nature and importance of holy living, and further observed that this was often done, oddly enough, in the name of real, vital, Christian faith. One way of expressing this different estimation of the essential fabric of the Christian life that emerged between Wesley and his "opponents" is in terms of the continuity between the old and new covenants and another in terms of law and gospel.

The usual way of stressing the discontinuity between the old and new covenants—a favorite device of antinomians—is to consider the former a covenant of works and the latter a covenant of grace, with the implication that the latter has utterly displaced the former. But this Wesley clearly and unequivocally disallows. In his sermon *The Lord Our Righteousness,* for example, he points out that both the Mosaic covenant and the covenant given by Christ are gracious, and that the covenant of works referred to by the Apostle Paul in a negative manner in his Epistle to the Romans concerns not Moses but only Adam in his unfallen state.[10] Neither the Hebrew people nor the church has ever been under a covenant of works. The movement from the Old Testament to the New is, therefore, one from grace to grace.

One reason why Wesley feared referring to the Mosaic covenant as one of works was because he realized that such a position could issue in a low estimation of the role of the moral law in the life of the believer, and could, in turn, detract from his emphasis on holy living. When this is done, the graciousness of the gospel is at times pitted against the moral law as if the former has largely if not utterly replaced the latter. Here, obedience to the law, keeping the commandments of God, is seen as either legality or as justification by works, and therefore as sub-Christian. But since—as has already been indicated in an earlier chapter—the moral law is holy, just, and good, the express image of God, and indicative of the immutable relationship between God and humanity, "it must remain in force, upon all mankind, and in all ages."[11] Christ, then, according to Wesley, has neither introduced a "new religion"[12] nor an "easier way to heaven"[13] in the sense that the moral and spiritual righteousness of the old covenant is repudiated. What has changed, however, is not the moral law itself, but the believer's relation to it; that is, the law is no longer fulfilled in a literal and external way, but in a new spiritual manner; its height and its depth, not fully appreciated by those under the old covenant, are now realized to a greater degree in all those who believe in Jesus Christ.

Moreover, Wesley noted the similarity between the covenants in terms of the relationship between the law and gospel itself. The moral law, simply put, is the gospel presented as a demand, and the gospel is the law presented as a promise.[14] In Wesley's own words, "the law (the moral not the ceremonial law) continually makes way for and points us to the gospel; on the other the gospel continually leads us to a more exact fulfilling of the law."[15] Such a posture is also expressed in the threefold use of the law that Wesley displays in his sermon *The Original, Nature, Properties and Use of the Law.* In this piece, concerning the third or the prescriptive use, Wesley writes, "The third use of the law is to keep us alive. It is the grand means whereby the blessed Spirit prepares the believer for larger communications of the life of God."[16] The law sends one to Christ, to be sure, but Christ also sends one back to the law for guidance and instruction. Both movements are integral to Wesley's assessment of the Christian life, and both are necessary to maintain his emphasis on faith *and* holy living, justification *and* sanctification.[17]

So concerned was Wesley with the specter of antinomianism, the teaching which makes the moral law void or of little consequence, that he produced two "tracts for the times" in 1750 to warn against this grave error. Indeed, it is highly probable that he had the teaching of such unabashed antinomians as William Cudworth and James Hervey in mind as he wrote these pieces.[18] In addition, as Albert Outler correctly observes, *The Law Established Through Faith: Discourse I and II,* although two separate sermons, actually comprise one extended essay and should be read together.[19] In fact, the structural relation between the two is perhaps best expressed in terms of a problem and solution model; that is, the problems raised in the first piece, the various ways of making void the law, are then countered in the second by showing how the law may yet be established by Christian faith.

The first and most usual way of making void the law through faith, as Wesley points out in *Discourse I,* is "not to preach the law at all."[20] Here, preaching the gospel is viewed as answering all the ends of the law, and, therefore, is deemed the principal, if not the sole, activity of preachers. The problem here, Wesley contends, is one of balance, for to preach Christ properly is "to preach all things that Christ hath spoken: all his promises; all his threatenings and commands; all that is written in his Book."[21] To neglect any aspect of this important ministry is to impoverish the saints. Thus in *Discourse II*—as one might expect—Wesley offers a solution to this first problem by admonishing his readers to establish the law by preaching it in its whole extent: in its height, depth, length, and breadth,[22] and by further exhorting them "to explain and enforce every part of it in the same manner as our great Teacher did while upon earth."[23] Such a task is necessary because Wesley believed that Christian congregations need to feed upon the inward spiritual meaning of the law; they need to look to the law as the face of God unveiled as humans are able to bear it, and they need to hear Christ preached in all His offices: as Priest and King, of course, but also as Prophet, if satisfying spiritual growth is to occur.

A second way of making void the law through faith is to teach that faith supersedes the necessity of holiness. When this is done, three things are usually assumed: first, that holiness is less necessary now than before Christ came;[24] second, that a lesser degree of it is necessary;[25] and third, that holiness is less necessary to believers than to others.[26] What lies behind such mistaken assumptions, as Wesley aptly observes, is a confused notion of Christian liberty where freedom is defined not in terms of freedom *from* the guilt and power of sin, and freedom *to* love God and neighbor, as it should be, but in terms of freedom from the law, works, and consequently, from holiness as well. For though none are justified by works of the law, such works are the inevitable fruit of real, vital faith. Wesley notes:

> "We are justified without the works of the law" as any previous condition of justification. But they are an immediate fruit of that faith whereby we are justified. So that if good works do not follow our faith, even all inward and outward holiness, it is plain our faith is nothing worth; we are yet in our sins.[27]

Interestingly enough, this second way of making the law void results from exaggerating the role of faith in the name of proper Christian doctrine and is therefore an error into which sincere and earnest Protestants may easily fall. The teaching of *sola fide* can quickly devolve into a doctrine of *solafidianism* if care is not taken to view faith, not as an end in itself, but as a gracious means to reestablish the law of love in human hearts. To be sure, Wesley taught that sinners are justified by faith as the only condition; nevertheless, he also affirmed that faith, though absolutely necessary, serves an instrumental role in the establishment of love. In other words, though faith is necessary and vital, it points beyond itself to the life of love and holiness. Faith is *in order to* love; it is the grand means to reestablish the law of love in human hearts. Wesley writes:

> In order to this we continually declare that faith itself, even Christian faith, the faith of God's elect, the faith of the operation of God, still is only the handmaid of love. As glorious and honourable as it is, it is not the end of the commandment. God hath given this honour to love alone. Love is the end of all the commandments of God.[28]

Wesley explores this relationship between faith and love in a second way, in terms of the temporal characteristics entailed, to show even more convincingly that love is the goal of the Christian life. Thus, he maintains in true Anglican fashion that faith is a temporary means which God has ordained to promote the eternal purpose of love.[29] Love, on the other hand, is quite different from faith in that it has existed before faith, even before the foundation of the world, and it will continue to exist after faith as well. Simply put, love is from eternity to eternity, but faith is not. Therefore, how mistaken a notion it is to blow faith out of all proportion so that it takes precedence over the eternal and immutable goal of the Christian life. "Faith is of no value in itself," Wesley warns, "yet as it leads to that end—the establishing anew the law of love in our hearts—it is on that account of unspeakable blessing to man, and of unspeakable value before God."[30] Faith will pass away, but love will never pass away.

The third, last, and most common way of making void the law through faith, Wesley states, "is the doing it practically; the making it void in *fact,* though not in *principle;* the living as if faith was designed to excuse us from holiness."[31] When the Christian life is lived in such a manner, it is supposed that less obedience is required under the grace of the gospel than under the law, and that one need not be so scrupulous and so rigorous as before. But these are two conclusions that cannot validly be drawn from the premises of justification by faith and the priority of God's grace. Wesley reasons, "Shall we be less obedient to God from filial love than we were from servile fear? Is love a less powerful motive than fear?"[32] And again he queries, "And have you not learned to say, 'Oh, I am not so scrupulous now," to which he responds with some measure of exasperation, "I would to God you were!"[33]

For Wesley, obedience to the moral law *is* required in the practical Christian life, not of course as the condition of acceptance, but in order to *continue* in the rich grace of God. Simply put, obedience to the moral law of God does not establish the Christian life, but is the necessary fruit of that faith which both justifies and sanctifies. If, for example, faith does not produce obedience to the moral law of God, works of charity and mercy, and holiness, it is clear to Wesley, at least, that such is a dead and not a living faith; it is a faith that is not being acted out in the world of God and neighbor, and is therefore all but useless. Indeed, in his piece *A Blow at the Root,* produced in 1762, Wesley rebukes all those antinomians who balk at their task and who look upon commandment-keeping as rank legality. He writes, "You can love him and keep his commandments; and to you his 'commandments are not grievous'. Grievous to them that believe! Far from it. They are the joy of your heart. Show then your love to Christ by keeping his commandments, by walking in all his ordinances blameless."[34]

Wesley was able to stress holiness and the law of God in the life of the believer precisely because of his doctrine of grace outlined above. The rich sanctifying grace of God which is the privilege of all believers is that grace which radically transforms a life by making it holy. Here the emphasis is not on imputation but on impartation. Believers are not simply "positionally" holy because of their relation to God—although this too is important—but they really are holy through God's sanctifying grace; they have been renewed in their innermost natures, transformed and cleansed by the Holy Spirit, and set at liberty to love God and neighbor. This, according to Wesley, is the great work which God does *in us*.[35] Sanctifying grace is real, potent, and effective; it has great consequence in the practical Christian life.

Because Wesley was ever mindful of God's initiating grace, he felt free to use a vocabulary in Christian discipleship that could easily, though without justification, give pause to some. He was not afraid, for instance, to use such words as "seek," "work," "strain," and "labor" in his spiritual counsel nor did he hesitate to urge those under his care to be obedient, fruitful, and even rigorous. Contrary to the claims of his opponents such as James Hervey, William Cudworth, and Augustus Toplady, Wesley was not a legalist who had forgotten the graciousness of the gospel. Instead, he was precisely the one who had considered the grace of God in a serious and thorough manner, and therefore was fully apprized of its tremendous enabling power with the resultant increase in responsibility. In short, the imperative mood did not drop out of Wesley's vocabulary. If anything, the grace of God intensified it.

PERSONAL ETHICS

It is interesting to note that many of the most lucid and able pieces on the subject of self-denial emerged from the pens of such Protestant divines as Richard Baxter, Jeremy Taylor, and William Law.[36] Neither Rome nor the Eastern Church held exclusive rights here. Indeed, self-denial was a "Protestant" topic in the seventeenth and eighteenth centuries especially among those groups, like the Puritans, who actively sought to preserve and pass on the genius of the Protestant Reformation. Yet, oddly enough, Wesley the Anglican appears to discount this rich heritage in a storm of criticism in his sermon *Self-Denial*. Among other things, he contends that previous (Protestant) writers had misunderstood the subject: "they did not see how exceeding broad this command is; or they were not sensible of the absolute, the indispensable necessity of it."[37] Moreover, Wesley maintains that earlier treatments never emerged from a sea of generalities to offer particular, very practical, and clear applications. These alleged deficiencies, then, become the main motivating factors behind this present sermon.

In *Self-Denial,* written in 1760, Wesley claims that various religious groups, for different reasons, have failed to understand properly the directive of Jesus: "If anyone would come after me, he must deny himself and take up his cross daily and follow me" (Luke 9:23). The predestinarians, for example, cry, "Salvation by works,"[38] when this saying is presented as a norm for the Christian life, and the antinomians charge that it is "preaching the law,"[39] as if self-denial and Christian experience were mutually exclusive. In light of such criticism, Wesley's principal task in this homily is to argue convincingly that a Christian can indeed practice self-denial, and that a Protestant can remain faithful to the graciousness of the gospel and yet engage in this rigorous spiritual discipline.

Perhaps part of the difference between Wesley and those who spoke harshly of self-denial consists in their different estimations of the phrase itself. The antinomians, for instance, may have immediately conjured up images of self-neglect, extreme mortification, and a morbid delight in suffering whenever it was used. For Wesley, however, the denial of self does not embrace those ascetic practices that are artificially contrived, self-inflicted, and which bear no necessary relation to living the Christian life such as "wearing a haircloth or iron girdles or anything else that would impair our bodily health."[40] Instead, self-denial is, quite simply, "the denying or refusing to follow our own will, from a conviction that the will of God is the only rule of action to us."[41]

In light of such a definition of self-denial, it is reasonable to infer that Wesley would have looked down upon many monastic practices, both ancient and modern, such as vows of silence, of location, and the like, and from all morbid and negative asceticism which bears little or no relation to the will of God. For this Anglican, only those disciplines which grow out of and foster obedience to the will of God are to be affirmed (so there is a place for prudential rules) but all else is deemed superfluous. It is not discipline for the sake of discipline nor suffering for the sake of suffering which matters, but the bearing of those things that cannot be avoided if the will of God is to be accomplished.

Closely associated with the issue of self-denial is that of taking up one's cross. These spiritual disciplines are not equivalent in the mind of Wesley, although he affirms the one should necessarily lead to the other. In the admonition of Jesus to take up our cross and follow Him, Wesley sees something higher, more demanding, than simply self-denial, for a cross encompasses what is actually contrary and displeasing to our nature, something which the denial of self does not necessarily entail. In short, the former unavoidably involves suffering; the latter does not. Wesley writes, "So that taking up our cross goes a little farther than denying ourselves; it rises a little higher, and is a more difficult task to flesh and blood, it being more easy to forego pleasure than to endure pain."[42]

The last distinction which Wesley draws in this sermon concerns the two attitudes in which the cross can be taken up. A cross can be borne passively, even reluctantly, or it can be actively embraced. With respect to the former manner he writes, "We are then properly said to bear our cross when we endure what is laid upon us without our choice, with meekness and resignation."[43] As noble as this response to the direction of God is, Wesley interjects that one may go even further than this in freely and willingly suffering what one is otherwise able to avoid.[44] Observe here that the emphasis on the concurrence of the will, the free assent to what is displeasing, calls for an active not a passive response to God's leading. One does not merely bear a cross; one actually, in a certain sense, welcomes it.

In Wesley's eyes, a life of self-denial and of taking up one's cross are crucial to all Christians of whatever tradition because they are integral to the promise and task of discipleship. In this present sermon, Wesley maintains that when one fails to follow Christ fully, it is always "owing to the want either of self-denial or taking up his cross."[45] Such a view expresses Wesley's judgment of the nature and process of the Christian life itself. In other words, Christian experience is not static, but dynamic; it is characterized by constant growth and movement. God continually calls His people forward, and if they do not respond to His grace, they do not remain where they are, as is mistakenly supposed, but actually regress. In fact, in *Self-Denial* Wesley delineates the slow and subtle process of descent into sin—what can be considered a reversal of the *ordo salutis* as referred to in a previous chapter—which is precipitated precisely by the reluctance to follow the leading of God in all things.[46] Not to go forward is to go backward; there is no standing still.

Clearly, it is no accident that Wesley places *Self-Denial* at the head of those sermons which deal largely with Christian personal ethics such as *The Cure of Evil Speaking, The Use of Money,* and *The Good Steward.* In many respects, the first sermon is foundational to the others; each succeeding piece develops, amplifies, and expresses the immense practicality of the first. Thus, for example, in *The Cure of Evil Speaking,* Wesley refers to refraining from this evil practice as an instance of self-denial in the following words: ". . .let this be the distinguishing mark of a Methodist: 'He censures no man behind his back: by this fruit ye may know him.' What a blessed effect of this self-denial should we quickly feel in our hearts.

How would our 'peace flow as a river', when we thus 'followed peace with all men'!"[47]

The theme of self-denial is even more apparent, however, in the latter parts of Wesley's sermon *The Use of Money*. But in the first section of this homily, it seems as if Wesley rejects his own spiritual counsel by urging the Methodists, interestingly enough, "to gain all you can,"[48] and those who are not well-schooled in the thought of Wesley, who see him as a dour, Puritanical figure are often surprised to learn this. That Wesley is consistent with his principles, self-denial being one of them, is evidenced by his observation drawn from the pages of the New Testament that it is the love of money, not money itself, which is the root of all evil; the fault lies not with the object but with the user. Accordingly, Wesley maintains that money is of "unspeakable service to all civilized nations in all the common affairs of life."[49] It is a blessed means to do great good: to bring the kingdom of God near to the poor, the homeless, and the despised. In the hands of the saints, it is an instrument of "doing all manner of good";[50] it is a means of grace to those in need. Small wonder, then, that he issues this first directive. Nevertheless, such encouragement to engage freely in the pursuit of money is nicely balanced by a few precautions: No persons, Wesley argues, may gain at the expense of the health of their own minds and bodies nor those of their neighbors.[51] But barring these precautionary remarks, the Methodists are left free to engage in commerce, to gain all that they can.

The chord of self-denial is struck more clearly in Wesley's second admonition to "save all you can."[52] The money gained under the first counsel, through a legitimate use of gifts and talents, is not to be squandered on the self; all needless expense is, therefore, to be cut off. Money should not be used to gratify the desires of the flesh, the desire of the eye, nor the pride of life. "Despise delicacy and variety, and be content with what plain nature requires,"[53] Wesley warns. In fact, so insistent was Wesley on this score that he demanded elsewhere that all who wished to remain members of the band societies must forsake the use of snuff and tobacco, not because they were injurious to health—the eighteenth century had little understanding of the toxic nature of these substances since they were often prescribed by physicians—but because they constituted "needless self-indulgence."[54]

A serious problem emerges, however, if these first two

rules are not complemented by a third. If a group of people like the Methodists is both industrious and frugal, the specter of wealth inevitably arises. Indeed, Wesley deems riches one of the most serious threats confronting his people, something that can insidiously transform the love of God and neighbor into a love of the world and self. In order to prevent this, he proposes a third step: having gained and saved all you can, now give all you can.[55] After proper but not excessive provision has been made for ourselves and our families we are to give as much as we are able.

The ground and reason for this third step lies in Wesley's doctrine of stewardship displayed in this sermon and also in *The Good Steward*. In these pieces, human beings are not presented as proprietors or owners, but as stewards of the many gifts and graces that the Lord has given them. God has entrusted people with talents of various sorts such as minds, bodies, money, health, influence and time, "but the sole property of these still rests in him."[56] Wesley writes, "As you yourself are not your own, but his, such is likewise all that you enjoy. Such is your soul, and your body—not your own, but God's. And so is your substance in particular."[57] Moreover, Wesley underscores in the latter sermon that we are stewards who one day will have to render an account. At the appointed time, God will judge our employment and improvement of all these things just enumerated.[58] None, therefore, are of an indifferent nature nor does any judicious employment of these gifts constitute a work of supererogation since all we can do is due to the Lord.[59]

It should be obvious by now that Wesley's first two rules concerning the use of money are part of a larger whole, and therefore should not be considered in isolation if distortion of his ethic is not to occur. Clearly, the first two rules are a means to an end; one gains and saves precisely in order to give. By these means people will be able to do the work of God in the world: to feed the hungry, to house the homeless, to clothe the naked—in short to bring about, at least in a small way, the kingdom of God on earth. Moreover, not to take this third step, to indulge in, feed, and thereby aggravate foolish desire is to impoverish the self, spiritually speaking, and to cut off one of the principal channels that God has established to shower His grace upon those in need.

SOCIAL ETHICS

In *Upon Our Lord's Sermon on the Mount: Discourse Four* Wesley endeavors to show that Christianity is essentially a social religion, that it prospers and finds its best expression in human communities, in the rough and tumble of life.[60] Remarkably enough, the chief tension which he has in mind in *Discourse Four* is not between personal and social religion, which is a modern concern, but between solitary and social religion. For Wesley, Christianity precludes, for instance, the practice of running off into the desert or the wilderness as the staple of Christian experience. And, by implication, the hermit's life characteristic of anchoretic monasticism as exemplified by St. Anthony of Egypt or the unstable Symeon Stylites,[61] appears to be repudiated as well. It should immediately be added, however, that Wesley does not condemn the "intermixing solitude or retirement with society,"[62] for this practice is often therapeutic when employed judiciously. The point is that one does not go to the wilderness to remain there. Moreover, this Anglican cleric is not adverse to some of the spiritual techniques of monasticism such as contemplation, but he is opposed to deeming it the "only way of worshipping God in spirit and in truth."[63] Wesley writes, "Therefore to give ourselves up entirely to this would be to destroy many branches of spiritual worship, all equally acceptable to God, and equally profitable, not hurtful, to the soul."[64]

Wesley so disapproves of solitary religion because it fails to provide its practitioners with the necessary environment for the promotion of such Christian virtues as mildness, gentleness, longsuffering, and peacemaking.[65] These "cannot possibly subsist without society,"[66] he claims, "without our living and conversing with other men."[67] Indeed, it is in the soil of difficult and perplexing relationships that the seed of patience flourishes; it is in the face of opposition to the kingdom that courage takes root. Or to use another analogy, society with its many problems, frustrations, and opportunities is the anvil upon which some of the greatest Christian graces are hammered out. But Wesley goes a step further and declares that "some intercourse even with ungodly and unholy men is absolutely needful in order to the full exertion of every temper which [Jesus Christ] has described as the way to the kingdom."[68]

Christians are not to love the world, to be sure; nevertheless, there is a real sense in which they need the world.

The social nature of Christianity is again emphasized by Wesley in his claim that it is impossible to conceal the religion of Jesus Christ. The deep, hidden, and profound work of the heart's renewal in the image and likeness of God cannot remain hidden, for it will inevitably be displayed in the life and works of Christians as they care for a hurting world. "Your holiness makes you as conspicuous as the sun in the midst of heaven,"[69] Wesley writes. And genuine Christian love cannot remain unrevealed anymore than light can.[70] To use a familiar Wesleyan phrase, faith works by love; inward religion, so mysterious and personal, is necessarily manifested in outward religion, in public life. Neither aspect can subsist without the other; both ingredients are necessary. "God hath joined them together,"[71] Wesley notes, "let not man put them asunder."[72]

In light of this close connection that Wesley draws between inward and outward religion, two errors are possible: On the one hand, if the interior life is merely stressed, faith will not achieve its proper end: namely, love. What will emerge, however, is a dead faith, the kind of spiritual narcissism that Wesley so rightly deplores in *Discourse IV*. But if, on the other hand, the inward life of the believer, the life of God in the soul, is not seen as the proper foundation for Christian activity in society, then the very heart, reason, and impetus for such activity will be obscured. Therefore, Wesley's social ethic should not be employed to repudiate or to undermine his emphasis on personal religion—that renewal of the believer's heart in righteousness and true holiness. His thought provides no warrant for this; in fact, it militates against it.

Since the basic structural relationship between inward and outward religion can be expressed in terms of a doctrine of revelation where the antecedent work of the believer's renewal, so mysterious and hidden, is manifested publicly, it is not surprising to learn that Wesley tracks the love of God and its rippling effects in two ever-widening circles: toward the church and toward the world. With respect to the first circle, Wesley wrote at least two sermons among the fifty-three whose principal point of departure is the character of the relations between believers. In *The Catholic Spirit,* for example, he examines the two grand hindrances that prevent the children of God from loving one another as they should: namely, that they can't all think alike or walk alike.[73] The basis of unity then among believers is not to be found in either opinions or in modes of worship; here each person must follow the dictates of his or her own conscience. Though Christians may be from different church traditions, though they may ascribe to various beliefs and practices, they can yet experience a profound unity in the love of God that has been shed abroad in their hearts. In 2 Kings 10:15, which is the text for this homily, Jehu does not inquire concerning Jehonadab's opinions or modes of worship, but simply asks, "Is thine heart right, as my heart is with thy heart?" (KJV)

Observe also that in *The Catholic Spirit* the basis for harmony is not in the diverse ministries that people undertake—for believers will divide on this point as well according to their convictions—but in that deep, gracious, and mysterious work that God has accomplished in the human soul. Listen to Wesley: "Is thy faith . . . filled with the energy of love?"[74] "Does the love of God constrain thee to serve him with fear?"[75] All of these queries then indicate, once again, that inward religion is not to be minimized; the love of God reigning in the human heart is the one common element in the midst of great diversity. In fact, no possibility for unity exists without it.

The obvious irenic tone of *The Catholic Spirit* should not be mistaken for either easy believism or cheap grace—to use the modern vocabulary. Wesley insists that the catholic spirit is not "speculative latitudinarianism."[76] It is not indifferent, therefore, to all opinions so that one teaching is deemed just as good as any other; this in Wesley's judgment is none other than the spawn of hell.[77] But neither is the catholic spirit "practical latitudinarianism."[78] It is not indifferent to modes of worship or to the choice of a congregation in which one is to live the Christian life.

Is Wesley then inconsistent with his earlier principle of catholicity? Not at all. But he is saying two things simultaneously. Believers should be firmly convinced concerning the opinions or the modes of worship they hold, always realizing, though, that other believers will not only differ, but will also be equally convinced of the rightness of their own judgments. Wesley's prescription, therefore, for satisfying relations within the larger church is conviction plus tolerance, and if the latter ingredient is not understood in light of the former, the prospect of a shallow, unprincipled faith undoubtedly emerges. Wesley cautions: "This unsettledness of thought, this being driven to and fro, and tossed about with every wind of doctrine, is a great curse, not a blessing; an irreconcilable enemy, not a friend, to true catholicism."[79] Thus, a mature faith is both tolerant and strongly held; there is no contradiction here.

Although there are many similarities between the sermons *The Catholic Spirit* and *A Caution Against Bigotry,* among which is a warning against dogmatism, there is at least one important difference. Whereas the former homily underscores the importance of the interior life in terms of holy love as a prerequisite for common life, the latter highlights the exterior life, the fruits which necessarily flow from a radically transformed heart. This shift in emphasis in *A Caution Against Bigotry* was precipitated, for the most part, by Wesley's apologetical purpose in this work. Several Anglican clergy, for example, John Toppin, the curate of Allendale in Northumberland among them, expressed disapproval with respect to Wesley's employment of lay preachers during the revival. In this polemic context, Wesley substantiates Methodist polity and practice in a number of ways: through an appeal to Scripture, apostolic practice, and reason. Nevertheless, the thrust of his argument seems to devolve upon the works that his lay preachers do and the resultant dissatisfaction of the Anglican clergy. Thus, bigotry is defined with an eye to the latter group as "too strong an attachment to, or fondness for, our own party, opinion, Church, and religion,"[80] so that we forbid those who cast out devils whom our Lord has not forbidden. Wesley writes, "Do you beware of this. Take care, first, that you do not convict yourself of bigotry by your unreadiness to believe that any man does cast out devils who differs from you. And if you are clear thus far, if you acknowledge the fact, then examine yourself. . . ."[81] So then in *The Catholic Spirit* different opinions and doctrines are not to spoil the love of God; in *A Caution Against Bigotry* they are not to spoil the work of God.

But the love of God is also manifested in a second circle: that is, toward the world. Such love can neither be contained nor exhausted in the first circle. In the sermon *The Reformation of Manners,* for example, preached by Wesley in 1763 under the auspices of the society by the same name, he displays his abiding concern for those who were beyond the walls of the church: the poor, the downtrodden, and the forgotten. In this endeavor, he followed in his father, Samuel's, footsteps who preached for this same society some sixty-five years earlier.[82]

Ostensibly, The Society for the Reformation of Manners was concerned with issues of public vice such as Sabbath breaking, drunkenness, gambling, prostitution, and the like. Apparently, this has led some to conclude that the substance of this homily "is one of the least evangelical of any of Wesley's sermons after 1738 . . . its conclusions are moralistic and hortatory."[83] Nevertheless, a different interpretation can and should be offered in light of the evidence within the sermon itself which strongly suggests that this is an "evangelical" sermon after all, especially since it flows naturally from Wesley's earlier emphasis of the inward renewal in love brought about by the grace of God. In the following quote from this sermon, for instance, notice the development and order pertaining to the circles of salvation. The reform of public life does not stand alone as an instance of moralism, isolated from Wesley's evangelical concerns; instead it is an integral part of a larger, gracious movement. Wesley writes:

> This is the original design of the church of Christ. It is a body of men compacted together in order, first, to save each his own soul, then to assist each other in working out their salvation, and afterwards, as far as in them lies, to save all men from present and future misery, to overturn the kingdom of Satan.[84]

Moreover, Wesley extols love in this sermon and argues for its indispensability in reforming activities: "And therefore it is highly expedient that all engaged therein have 'the love of God shed abroad in their hearts'; that they should all be able to declare, we love him, because he first loved us."[85] The elimination of public vice then is a clear manifestation of the love of God; it is not less than the gospel but is at the very heart of the good news of freedom from all that oppresses the human spirit or detracts from its dignity. So in this sermon, Wesley boldly exhorts all Christians "to join together in order to oppose the works of darkness, to spread the knowledge of God their Saviour, and to promote his kingdom upon earth,"[86] and it is in these activities as well that the light of the gospel is revealed. Quite simply, the reformation of manners is one of the ways the gospel is revealed in a broader arena, in a sinful public context. The dictum here, as elsewhere for Wesley, is that works are preceded by empowering grace, and that grace is ever active in all manner of works, both public and private. Once again, the continuity between these ingredients is striking.[87]

NOTES

[1] Outler, *Works,* 3:545. (*Free Grace*) But notice that Calvin, and Luther for that matter, would never have agreed to Wesley's further emphasis that grace is free for all. Such a position would undermine both Calvin's predestination and Luther's bondage of the will which issues in the idea of predestination as well. Cf. McNeill, *Institutes,* 1:920ff., and E. Gordon Rupp and Philip S. Watson, eds., *Luther and Erasmus: Free Will and Salvation* (Philadelphia: The Westminster Press, 1969), pp. 223ff.

[2] Ibid., 1:117. (*Salvation by Faith*)

[3] Ibid., 3:207. (*On Working Out Our Own Salvation*)

[4] Ibid., p. 208.

[5] Ibid.

[6] Ibid.

[7] Ibid.

[8] Ibid., p. 207.

[9] William Ragsdale Cannon, *The Theology of John Wesley* (Nashville: Abingdon-Cokesbury Press, 1946), p. 116.

[10] Outler, *Works,* 1:202. (*The Lord Our Righteousness*)

[11] Ibid., p. 552. (*Sermon on the Mount, V*)

[12] Ibid., p. 551.

[13] Ibid.

[14] Ibid. p. 554.

[15] Ibid.

[16] Ibid., 2:16. (*The Original, Nature, Properties, and Use of the Law*) Compare Wesley's third prescriptive use with that of John Calvin in the latter's *Institutes.* Cf. McNeil, *Institutes,* 1:360ff.

[17] It is interesting to note that in his *Lectures on Galatians* Martin Luther listed only two formal uses for the law: a political and a theological one. The function of the first is to restrain the wicked who care nothing for Christian principles, while the role of the second is to drive the sinner to Christ through its accusatory force. Since Luther considered the theological or the accusatory use of the law as primary in importance, this led him to view the relation between law and gospel not so much in terms of continuity, as Wesley saw fit, but in terms of a dialectical tension. Thus, Luther was able to speak of "a time of the law" and a "time of the gospel" which signifies that the process of salvation is characterized by movement. In one place in his *Lectures on Galatians* he even stated, "Then let the Law withdraw; for it was indeed added for the sake of disclosing and increasing transgressions, but only

until the point when the offspring would come. Once He is present, let the law stop. . . ." Cf. Martin Luther, *Luther's Works,* ed., Jaroslav Pelikan, Vol. 26: *Lectures on Galatians, 1535* (St. Louis: Concordia Publishing House, 1963), pp. 308–09, 317.

[18]Outler, *Works,* 2:1.

[19]Ibid., p. 3.

[20]Ibid., p. 22. (*The Law Established Through Faith, I*)

[21]Ibid., p. 25.

[22]Ibid., p. 35. See also Wesley's letter "To an Evangelical Layman" written most probably to Ebenezer Blackwell on 20 December 1751. Cf. Frank Baker, *Wesley's Works,* 26:482–89.

[23]Ibid., p. 34.

[24]Ibid., p. 26.

[25]Ibid.

[26]Ibid.

[27]Ibid., p. 28.

[28]Ibid., p. 38. (*The Law Established Through Faith, II*)

[29]Ibid., p. 39.

[30]Ibid., pp. 40–41.

[31]Ibid., p. 29. (*The Law Established Through Faith, I*)

[32]Ibid., pp. 30–31.

[33]Ibid., p. 31.

[34]Jackson, *Wesley's Works,* 10:369. This form of antinomianism is a contemporary danger as well. How many Christian books today belittle the importance of obeying the law of God, of keeping commandments, and other ways of exercising the obedience of faith as if these things detracted from a sound and mature faith.

[35]Outler, *Works,* 2:187. (*The New Birth*) See also *Justification by Faith* 1:187.

[36]Ibid. 2:236.

[37]Ibid. p. 239. (*Self-Denial*) See also Outler's comment, note number three, p. 240, that this constitutes a generalization.

[38]Ibid., p. 241. See also Outler's note number six.

[39]Ibid.

[40]Ibid., p. 245.

[41]Ibid., p. 242.

[42]Ibid., p. 243.

[43]Ibid., p. 244.

[44]Ibid.

[45]Ibid., p. 245.

[46]The notion that Wesley considered the Christian walk as one of process and development, that the directive is always "Go forward!" is amply argued and illustrated in Clarence Bence's dissertation, "John Wesley's Teleological Hermeneutic." University Microfilms, 1981.

[47]Outler, *Wesley's Works,* p. 262. (*The Cure of Evil-Speaking*)

[48]Ibid., p. 268. (*The Use of Money*)

[49] Ibid.

[50] Ibid.

[51] Ibid., pp. 269–73.

[52] Ibid., p. 273.

[53] Ibid., p. 274.

[54] Jackson, *Wesley's Works,* 8:274. On this point, irony abounds simply because contemporary prohibitions often focus on the medical problem entailed, and forget that this was principally an issue of self-denial for Wesley. Modern Methodists, for example, often take pride in their abstinence from tobacco products while at the same time some of them live in relative luxury! Such followers clearly miss Wesley's basic principle.

[55] Outler, *Wesley's Works,* 2:277. (*The Use of Money*)

[56] Ibid., Cf. Jackson, *Wesley's Works,* 8:269–71. Notice that the Rules of the United Societies also evidence the need and importance of doing as much good as one can as well as the self-denial and the stewardship that makes all of this possible.

[57] Ibid.

[58] Ibid., pp. 293ff. (*The Good Steward*)

[59] Ibid., p. 297.

[60] Ibid., 1:533. (*Upon Our Lord's Sermon on the Mount: Discourse IV*)

[61] One of the practices employed by Symeon Stylites was to bind himself in ropes so tightly that they cut through to his bones with the result that the ropes could be removed only by causing extreme pain. This was also the same person who tried to achieve holiness by sitting on the top of a pole for thirty-six years. Cf. Philip Schaff, *History of the Christian Church,* (Grand Rapids: Wm. B. Eerdmans Publishing Company, 1910), 3:191ff.

[62] Ibid., p. 534.

[63] Ibid., p. 544.

[64] Ibid.

[65] Ibid., p. 534.

[66] Ibid., p. 535.

[67] Ibid.

[68] Ibid., p. 536. (Bracketed material mine)

[69] Ibid., p. 539.

[70] Ibid., p. 543.

[71] Ibid.

[72] Ibid.

[73] Outler, *Wesley's Works,* 1:82. (*The Catholic Spirit*)

[74] Ibid., p. 88.

[75] Ibid. The exemplar of the catholic spirit that Wesley holds up in the standard sermons is none other than George Whitefield. This is interesting, especially in light of the fact that the two had a falling out

WESLEY ON SALVATION

after Wesley published his sermon, *Free Grace*. Cf. Outler, *Works,* 2:344–45. (*On the Death of George Whitefield*)

[76] Ibid., p. 92.
[77] Ibid.
[78] Ibid., p. 93.
[79] Ibid., pp. 92–93.
[80] Ibid., p. 76. (*A Caution Against Bigotry*)
[81] Ibid., pp. 76–77.
[82] Outler, *Works,* 2:300. (*The Reformation of Manners*)
[83] Ibid., 2:301.
[84] Ibid., p. 302. Granted, Wesley does not underscore justification by faith, nor does he name the grace of Christ very often in this sermon; nevertheless, the content of this piece must be understood in line with Wesley's evangelical emphases which, in a sense, are presupposed.
[85] Ibid., p. 314.
[86] Ibid., p. 301.
[87] Wesley's emphasis on social religion has often been misappropriated by those contemporary theologians who are largely interested in a radical critique of social and political institutions, and who, therefore, often call for the kinds of broad structural changes in the social order of which Wesley, an eighteenth-century thinker, was only dimly aware. Although Wesley was clearly an aggressive reformer, tackling the problems of unemployment, slavery, poverty, ignorance, and war, his thought was, after all, more conducive to the liberal reform characteristic of his pre-Marxist and pre-social-gospel age. In other words, although the father of Methodism was a reformer, he was not a revolutionary, and those Methodist theologians like Jose Miguez Bonino who closely identify Christianity and socialism will find little to feed upon in Wesley's social ethics. In short, that Wesley considered Christianity a social religion does not constitute a green light to translate, without much ado, his eighteenth-century thought into a contemporary agenda. One must first of all note—and note it well—what Wesley meant by "social religion." Cf. Miguez Bonino, "Wesley's Doctrine of Sanctification From a Liberationist Perspective," in *Sanctification and Liberation,* ed. Theodore Runyon (Nashville: Abingdon Press, 1981), pp. 55ff., and Kenneth J. Collins, "John Wesley and Liberation Theology: A Closer Look," *The Asbury Theological Journal,* Vol. 42, Num. 1 (Spring 1987) 85–90.

VI

PROBLEMS AND POSSIBILITIES OF THE CHRISTIAN LIFE: Subsequent Repentance and Christian Perfection

TEMPTATIONS AND SPIRITUAL DARKNESS

Anyone who has ever read even the briefest part of Wesley's Journal should realize that he was sincere, realistic, and frank about his own spiritual progress. In these pages and in his letters, he appears before us—to use the words of Frank Baker—"warts and all."[1] This remarkable candor of Wesley, especially when he describes some of his more somber moods, has sometimes been used against him. Thus, for example, Theodore Jennings argues that Wesley's spiritual malaise after Aldersgate utterly detracts from that experience, rendering it a "non-event."[2] But where in Wesley's writings did he ever state that the new birth cannot be followed by temptations, doubts, or fears? Moreover, where did he ever state that the Christian walk would be one great success story from beginning to end, a march from joy to joy, from spiritual exaltation to even greater exaltation? Wesley's nineteenth-century heirs might have fashioned such a rose garden, but clearly he did not.

In 1760, Wesley, with painstaking honesty, produced a sermon entitled, *Heaviness Through Manifold Temptations,* which displays the difficulty and the anything-but-easy challenge of the Christian life. In this piece, he maintains that spiritual heaviness is not inconsistent with regenerating faith and Christian status. Indeed, one may experience acute trial and spiritual heaviness and yet exercise faith, hope, and love, and have a measure of peace and joy in the Holy Spirit, even inward and outward holiness. Clearly, this portion of the sermon is autobiographical, for on 26 May 1738, two days after his

Aldersgate experience, Wesley wrote in his Journal, "My soul continued in peace, but yet in heaviness because of manifold temptations."[3] And a few days later, he observed, "I was so strongly assaulted by one of my old enemies, that I had scarce strength to open my lips. . . . But after I had prayed, faintly, as I could, the temptation vanished away."[4]

The error that vibrant Christian spirituality is inconsistent with spiritual heaviness becomes even more apparent, however, when the causes of such heaviness—any of which are clearly unavoidable—are considered. Bodily disorders, Wesley observes, such as acute diseases, violent pain, consumption, and nervous disorders can weigh heavily on the spirit.[5] Faith neither overturns the course of nature here nor does it "hinder the sinking of the spirits."[6] Likewise, poverty, the death of a loved one, or the apostasy of a close friend can cause such anguish of spirit as to try severely even the heartiest soul. Furthermore, a far deeper, clearer, and fuller knowledge of inbred sin, that corruption of our nature which yet remains after the new birth, can—but does not necessarily—bring us into heaviness.[7] And in all these circumstances, Wesley cautions, "We may be assured our great adversary will not be wanting to improve his opportunity."[8]

But why do the children of God experience such heaviness at all? In other words, why does a providential God allow this unenviable situation to occur? These temptations are allowed to buffet believers, Wesley argues, precisely in order to test and improve their faith, even as gold is tested and improved by fire.[9] The dross is burnt up in the heat of affliction, so to speak, leaving a refined and strengthened faith. Beyond this, manifold temptations can confirm and increase our hope; they can advance our love of both God and neighbor, and, lastly, they can foster our growth in holiness of heart and life. They are, therefore, not for our destruction or punishment as some may suppose, but for our spiritual growth and improvement.

A second spiritual condition, however, which Wesley portrays in his sermons is the wilderness state. It is markedly different from the one just described in that it is inconsistent with the graces of regeneration and Christian status; in short, it is a state of abject sin and spiritual darkness. Indeed, the nature of the wilderness state, unlike spiritual heaviness, entails a loss of that faith which God once wrought in believing hearts.[10] Darkness is again "on the face of their souls," Wesley writes, "and blindness on the eyes of their understanding."[11] More-over, it appears that Wesley's choice of the phrase "wilderness state" in this context is most appropriate since such an image conjures up the rebellion, murmurings, and aimless wanderings of the ancient Israelites, aspects which seem to be equally descriptive, spiritually speaking, of those Christians who once knew the sanctifying grace of God in its purity and power, but who are now mired in sin.

The wilderness state, however, is not only one of darkness but also of alienation, for when the chord of faith is severed, this necessarily involves the loss of love as well "which cannot but rise or fall at the same time, and in the same proportion, with true, living faith."[12] As noted earlier, there is an inseparable connection, for Wesley, between faith and love. Faith is in order to love, and therefore those who are deprived of the means of faith are equally deprived of the ends of love. But not only are faith and love inextricably tied, many of the other spiritual virtues are as well. In fact, Wesley affirms the interrelatedness of several spiritual virtues throughout this homily, with a kind of domino effect. The loss of faith, for example, implies the loss of love, which in turn implies the loss of joy, which results in the loss of peace until finally, power over sin is also forfeited.

With little doubt, the causes of the wilderness state, this estrangement from God, are various. Wesley lists them, however, under three main headings: sin, ignorance, and temptation. Under the first heading, Wesley contends that both sins of commission such as anger, foolish desire and the like, and sins of omission such as neglect of private prayer, failure to rebuke our sinning neighbors, etc., will estrange us from the life of God. If this is the nature of the malady, then the spiritual counsel should be one which highlights repentance. But if, on the other hand, the general cause of this darkness is ignorance so that believers erroneously think that all the children of God must at some point in their experience go through this state of darkness, then one must counter these false notions with a knowledge of the Holy Scriptures. Lastly, if the general cause is temptation which takes one unaware due to spiritual pride or sloth, and which in addition causes one to despair and to descend into sin, then one must teach believers that temptation need not result in despair or sin and that one must always expect temptation as the normal course in the Christian life since we

111

dwell, to use the words of Wesley, "in an evil world, among wicked, subtle, malicious spirits."[13]

In his sermons, *Heaviness Through Manifold Temptations* and *The Wilderness State,* Wesley obviously takes great pains to display in rich detail two of the more troublesome spiritual conditions which were the concern of many of the people in the Methodist societies. But in these homilies, he displays even greater concern to keep distinct these two states just described. Spiritual darkness or the wilderness state implies a weakening if not a total loss of joy, peace, and the love of God whereas heaviness does not. The two, therefore, are not to be confused. Wesley cautions: ". . . as long as we can distinguish faith from unbelief, hope from despair, peace from war, the love of God from the love of the world, we may infallibly distinguish heaviness from darkness."[14]

Again, there may be a need for heaviness for a brief period as a time of trial and as a goad to the further appropriation of grace, but there can be no need for spiritual darkness. Indeed, it is the prerogative of Christians, so long as they remain in sanctifying faith, to live constantly above such spiritual darkness. Great care should therefore be taken, Wesley advises, to make sure that our manifold temptations lead not to our spiritual impoverishment—through an unnecessary descent into the wilderness state—but to our spiritual enrichment.

Nevertheless, for Wesley, there is no spiritual state no matter how lofty from which one is unable to fall. This maxim has two important implications. First, the fact that one has been regenerated does not eliminate the possibility of future sin or even eventual damnation. Though believers have received the sanctifying grace of God, this does not necessarily mean that they will continue in it. Truly, if there is a sense of security in Wesley's theology—and there most certainly is—it is not found here. One must not only make a good start, but one must also continue and persevere in the grace of God. It is not a matter of once in grace, always in grace.

Second, entering into a state of sin and darkness by believers does not constitute proof that they were never "truly" born of God as some theologies teach. For Wesley, it simply means that such unfortunates have fallen from the rich grace of God and they, therefore, need to do the first works of repentance with its fruits until they are reestablished in faith. Observe here as elsewhere that part of the genius of Wesley's theology consists in its remarkable ability to hold two notions in dialectical tension: realism concerning human behavior on the one hand, and the very highest standards of Christian faith and practice on the other.

INBRED SIN

Though a far deeper and fuller knowledge of inbred sin can result in spiritual heaviness, as indicated earlier, such knowledge is absolutely necessary for spiritual maturity. Without it, one runs the risk of a presumption and a naïvefe which will topple under the strokes of the carnal nature, possibly bringing down with it one's faith as well. To prevent such a calamity, Wesley instructed the Methodists concerning the two-fold nature of sin which entails both an act and a state of being or what in other places he referred to as outward sin and inward sin respectively. Note that the issue here is not whether a child of God commits outward sin or not, for as Wesley states, "We all agree and earnestly maintain, 'He that committeth sin is of the devil,' "[15] the issue is whether any inward sin remains in those who believe. Put another way, the question is this: "Is a justified or regenerate man freed from *all sin* as soon as he is justified? Is there then no sin in his heart?"[16]

In his sermon *On Sin in Believers,* which was preached in 1763, Wesley answers this important question in the negative. In support of his argument, he marshals a number of sources among which are the primitive church, Scripture, experience, and reason.[17] Concerning the first witness, that of the primitive church, Wesley affirms that "the whole body of ancient Christians declare with one voice that even believers in Christ, till they are strong in the Lord . . . have need to wrestle with flesh and blood, with an evil nature."[18] More particularly, he refers to his own Anglican Church which declares in her ninth Article of Religion that the "infection of nature doth remain, yea, in them that are regenerated."[19] And to further his case, Wesley points out that the Greek, Roman, and Reformed churches are all in agreement here. In other words, there is universal testimony from the major church traditions on this matter.

Though Wesley in this sermon begins with the witness of the primitive church, this indicates merely chronological and not valuational priority. Wesley, being the good Protestant that

113

he was, naturally gives Scripture first rank. And in his handling of the Bible, he focuses on the New Testament, especially on the writings of the Apostle Paul. Indeed, the notion that believers are freed from all sin the moment they believe is repudiated by Paul, so Wesley reasons, in the Apostle's teaching that the flesh lusts against the spirit and the spirit against the flesh (Gal. 5:17). Moreover, Wesley cites Paul's First Letter to the Corinthians to show that the latter acknowledged two contrary principles in the hearts of believers, that they could be spiritual and to a certain extent carnal at the same time.

As the erroneous doctrine of sinless babes in Christ is contrary to tradition and Scripture so is it also contrary to the experience of the children of God. "These continually feel an heart bent to backsliding," Wesley contends, "a natural tendency to evil, a proneness to depart from God, and to cleave to the things of earth."[20] Thus, on the one hand, believers are sensible of pride, self-will, and unbelief; yet at the same time they know that they are in fact the children of God which they cannot doubt for a moment.[21] But how is it that Christ can be in the same heart where sin is? Wesley explains that Christ cannot reign where sin reigns nor where sin is allowed, but the Lord can and does dwell in the heart that is fighting against all sin.[22]

A few distinctions concerning the nature of sin are in order so that the preceding will be properly understood. First, as was alluded to in passing, believers are free from both the guilt (justification) and power (regeneration) of sin, but not from the being of it. Wesley writes, "That believers are delivered from the guilt and power of sin we allow; that they are delivered from the being of it we deny."[23] The point is that sin has no more dominion over the believer, but it still exists. Second, great havoc results when these distinctions are blurred, especially as concerns Wesley's doctrine of Christian perfection. When this is done, it is often argued that those perfected in love are the only ones who are free from the guilt and power of sin, but according to Wesley, properly speaking, such spiritual liberty is characteristic even of the regenerate. Clearly, then, this type of error is indicative of the generally low estimate, which is prevalent today, of *both* entire sanctification and the new birth.[24]

To be sure, one of the great dangers which lurks on the horizon for believers is that of undervaluing the work of justification and the new birth in the anticipation of a further work of grace: namely, Christian perfection. This is the grand device of Satan, Wesley points out, since the motive involved appears to be so noble—that of an earnest desire to be perfect in love—but which is soon perverted into other courses such as faithlessness and despair. Just how is such a transition brought about? In his sermon *Satan's Devices,* Wesley cites a number of ways in which Satan operates in order to retard, spoil, or even eliminate the faith of the children of God. First, this evil power endeavors "to damp our joy in the Lord by the consideration of our own vileness, sinfulness, [and] unworthiness."[25] The measure of joy which properly pertains to the children of God is thus robbed through a consideration of the sin which yet remains.[26]

Second, as Satan attempts to rob believers of joy so also does he seek to rob them of peace. He continually pricks the conscience with such barbs as "God is holy; you are unholy,"[27] and "How is it possible that you, unclean as you are, should be in a state of acceptance with God?"[28] If ground is given here, believers run the risk of losing faith, of doubting that they ever were accepted of God, with the likely consequence that they will seek something *in themselves* as the basis of their acceptance. This will result in an overturning of the very foundation of Christian faith.

Third, Wesley notes in this sermon that Satan often quotes Scripture to believers in order to cast a pall over what they have already attained, by asking such questions as, "Is it not the word of him that cannot lie, 'Without holiness no man shall see the Lord'?"[29] Since believers know that they are still in some measure unholy, such a question can strike the conscience hard and engender fearful doubt. Satan continues the assault by attacking the righteousness of believers and by endeavoring to destroy their faith. If this is done, it will "tear up the very root of the whole work of God,"[30] for without faith it is impossible to be holy. It is then that the ultimate design of this evil power will have been regrettably achieved.

But in this sermon, *Satan's Devices,* Wesley not only focuses on the machinations of Satan, but also on some of the psychological and spiritual characteristics of believers which prove to be particularly problematic. Thus, for example, when he writes that the children of God "were so taken up with what they were to receive hereafter as utterly to neglect what they had already received,"[31] this serves to highlight the ingratitude for existing grace, the impatience toward future grace, and the lack of humility which undergirds it all. Wesley comments, "In expectation of having five talents more, they buried their one talent in the earth. At least they did not improve it as they might have done to the glory of God and the good of their own souls."[32]

The way, then, through this special kind of trial, so fraught with danger, is marked by vigilance. The more that believers feel their inbred sin, "the more [they must] rejoice in confident hope that all this shall be done away."[33] Upon the realization that they are yet unholy, the children of God must cling to the promise that they have been freely justified by God's grace, and that they are, indeed, acceptable in His sight. And lastly, believers, Wesley cautions, must "stir up the gift of God" which is in them and "never let that slip."[34] In other words, this is a time not for timidity but for boldness, not for murmuring against God but for the confident realization that yet a little while, if one remains faithful and improves the grace already bestowed, the burden of sin "shall be clean gone."[35]

SUBSEQUENT REPENTANCE

In Chapter 2, it was observed that Wesley understands repentance basically in terms of self-knowledge, as "knowing ourselves sinners, yea, guilty, helpless sinners. . . ."[36] But since he defines sin in terms of both act and being, the self-knowledge entailed in repentance will therefore come in more than one form. Not surprisingly then, Wesley writes, "Repentance is of two sorts; that which is termed legal, and that which is styled evangelical repentance. The former is a thorough conviction of sin; the latter is a change of heart from all sin to all holiness."[37] The first sort of repentance is necessary at the very beginning of the Christian walk; the second in the midst of it. Again, one is a "conviction of our utter sinfulness and guiltiness and helplessness, and precedes our receiving [the] kingdom of God."[38] The other is required "after we have believed the gospel."[39]

In his sermon *The Repentance of Believers* written in 1767, Wesley thoroughly explores the idea of subsequent repentance under three headings: First, this repentance, unlike the previous one, involves a conviction of all the sin remaining in our hearts such as pride, self-will, and love of the world. Second, it includes a conviction of the guiltiness of the children of God which, Wesley cautions, must be understood in a peculiar sense:

> For it is certain, "there is no condemnation for them that are in Christ Jesus" . . . Yet can they no more bear the strict justice of God now than before they believed. This pronounces them to be still worthy of death on all the preceding accounts. And it would absolutely condemn them thereto, were it not for the atoning blood. Therefore, they are thoroughly convinced that they still deserve punishment, although it is hereby turned aside from them.[40]

Third, a conviction of utter helplessness is another aspect of this repentance. By this, Wesley means two things. Believers, by themselves, are no more able to do good works than before they were justified; instead, a moment by moment dependence on God and His grace is emphasized.[41] Moreover, by helplessness is meant, "an absolute inability to deliver ourselves from that guiltiness or desert of punishment whereof we are still conscious."[42]

It should be apparent by now that the evangelical repentance of which Wesley writes concerns the carnal nature, the inbred (original) sin which remains in the hearts even of believers, that was spelled out so clearly in his earlier sermons *On Sin in Believers* and *Satan's Devices*. To be sure, Wesley learned from many quarters that all sin is not removed in one grand stroke the moment one believes. Instead, the Lord must speak "the second time, 'Be clean'."[43] And if there is no second change or repentance, he declares, "We must be content to remain full of sin till death."[44]

CHRISTIAN PERFECTION

Interestingly enough, the two sermons *On Sin in Believers* and *The Repentance of Believers* are actually about Christian perfection in the sense that they highlight the sin which still remains and which constitutes the chief obstacle to perfect love. In other words, these homilies approach this subject in a negative fashion by showing what yet prevents the fullest realization of God's grace. But Wesley also considered the subject positively, not by stressing the removal of sin but by depicting the very heart, the essence, of Christian perfection in his description of holy love in a few of his more important sermons.

One of Wesley's earliest sermons on Christian perfection is *The Circumcision of the Heart* which was preached at St. Mary's Oxford on 1 January 1733. It should come as no surprise to learn that his understanding of holiness in this piece is rather mature and well developed. His readings in the works of Taylor, à Kempis, and William Law in the third decade of the eighteenth century no doubt had prepared him for this. What is remarkable, however, is his inclusion of humility (repentance) among the three cardinal virtues of faith, hope, and love. Such inclusion seems to be an early emphasis which is not duplicated in his later works, especially since it might be seen as detracting from *sola fide*.

At any rate, *The Circumcision of the Heart* makes a significant contribution to the understanding of Wesley's doctrine of Christian perfection in that it views the latter positively in terms of holy tempers; it is—to use Wesley's own words—a "habitual disposition of the soul"[45] and entails being endued with "those virtues which were in Christ Jesus."[46] It describes, in other words, the characteristics of holy love reigning in the human heart, a love which excludes all sin.

But perhaps Wesley's best and most lucid description of Christian perfection is found in his sermon by the same name which he preached in 1741. Without doubt, the doctrinal emphasis here was greatly misunderstood by many people, including Moravians and Calvinistic Methodists alike, and so Wesley takes great pains in this work to indicate first of all what Christian perfection is not and then, second, to describe what it is. Concerning the former, he observes first of all that Christians are not perfect in knowledge. Freedom from all ignorance is not promised to those who utterly embrace the love of God. Believers must continue to study and learn and even then the mysteries of the Trinity and the Incarnation, for example, will escape their clearest thoughts.[47]

Second, since those who are perfected in love are not free from ignorance, neither can they be free from all mistakes, at least in terms of things unessential to salvation. They will continue to err concerning the character of people—judging them better or worse than they should—and in terms of the interpretation of the Bible.[48] Simply put, no believer at any time is either infallible or omniscient.

Third, Christians are not so perfect as to be free from infirmities: that is, from "weakness or slowness of understanding, dullness or confusedness of apprehension, incoherency of thought, irregular quickness or heaviness of imagination."[49] What Wesley probably has in mind here is the interaction between the body and the soul and the resultant confusion of thought that can occur due to limitations of the body in terms of fatigue, illness, or physiologically based disorders. But note that an infirmity is not a license to sin nor can it ever be used as an excuse for sin. It is simply an amoral temporal limitation expressive of human finiteness.

Fourth, perfect love does not eliminate temptation. The Bible does not promise believers that they will be free from temptation to sin. Instead, as noted earlier and as Wesley correctly observes, the Scriptures repeatedly exhort all believers to remain steadfast in the face of manifold temptations. Perfection defined as freedom from trial, then, "belongeth not to this life."[50] So if this is what is hoped for, the hope is in vain.

Last, Wesley rejected the idea of a perfection of degrees, a perfection that would not admit of a continual increase and advance as one improves the rich grace of God. Thus, there is no place in this revivalist's theology for the notion that one has arrived spiritually. Those whose hearts have been made pure by the blood of Christ must continue to grow. Christian perfection, so understood, is not static but dynamic, not a "perfected perfection" as Outler correctly points out, but a "perfecting perfection."[51] "How much soever any man hath attained, or in how high a degree soever he is perfect," Wesley warns, "he hath still need to grow in grace, and daily to advance in the knowledge and love of God his Savior."[52] There is no room for spiritual elitism here nor for spiritual complacency.

It is in the second part of the sermon *Christian Perfection* that Wesley finally considers in what sense believers can legitimately hope to be perfect. To facilitate this discussion, he draws heavily from the First Letter of John and appeals to the epistle's distinction between little children, young men, and fathers as an example of spiritual growth and also as a way to highlight the several stages of the Christian life. Properly speaking, however, Wesley is chiefly concerned with "the fathers"[53] in this discourse, although he does elaborate to a considerable degree on the prerogatives of the first two stages as will be evident shortly.

119

Indeed, although few scholars have noted this, Wesley spends a good deal of the remaining material in this sermon defending, through a careful use of Scripture, his understanding of what constitutes a Christian, a child of God. "Even babes in Christ," he writes, "are in such a sense perfect as, first, not to commit sin."[54] Again, those who are justified in the lowest sense, "do not continue in sin."[55] But why is this material here? Why is it included in this context of Christian perfection? Wesley probably elaborated on these points because he feared that the normal privilege of all believers would be confused with that of those perfected in love—to the detriment of both. Subsequent Methodist history, both British and American, proved that Wesley's fears were not ill-founded.

Continuing his main line of thought of what constitutes Christian perfection, Wesley asserts that the graces of mature Christians, those who are "strong in the Lord,"[56] exceed those of babes in Christ in at least two respects: first, they are free from evil thoughts; second, they are delivered from evil tempers. Concerning the former, Wesley reasons this way: if the heart is no longer evil, then evil thoughts involving ill-will, lust, or envy will not proceed from it. Though believers may still be tempted by such thoughts, they will not yield to them. In addition, Wesley wrote an important sermon in 1762 entitled *Wandering Thoughts* in which he describes two classes of thoughts: those which wander from God and those which wander "from the particular point we have in hand,"[57] the one sinful, the other not. Since the first thoughts constitute practical atheism for Wesley, a heart of unbelief, one can expect to be free from them. He writes:

> What kind of wandering thoughts are sinful, and what not, is the third thing to be inquired into. And, first, all those thoughts which wander from God, which leave him no room in our minds, are undoubtedly sinful . . . Such are all murmuring, discontented thoughts, which say, in effect, "We will not have thee to rule over us"; all unbelieving thoughts, whether with regard to his being, his attributes, or his providence.[58]

But one can never be released from wandering thoughts in the second sense, in terms of those which stray from the point one has in mind. And these are no more sinful, Wesley notes, "than the motion of the blood in our veins."[59]

What is especially noteworthy about Wesley's claim that only those who are sanctified wholly are free from evil tempers is not the restriction of this freedom to the mature in faith, but the stress on a real change, in terms of holy tempers, in the hearts of believers. Naturally, this means that salvation is not simply a forensic exchange in the sense that people are declared to be other than they are—declared saints but in reality sinners—instead salvation involves actual renewal, transformation, and purification through the ever-potent grace of God. It is the difference, once again, between imputation and impartation that is evident here, and whenever the leading motif in the discussion is sanctification, whether initial or entire, it is the theme of impartation which characteristically predominates.

Just what are the tempers which mark the sanctified? Taking 1 John 3:3 as his guide, Wesley attests that the wholly sanctified are purified from pride, self-will, and anger,[60] precisely because Christ was lowly of heart, desired only to do the will of His Father, and was meek and humble.[61] In other words, the benefits of Christ fall upon believers in this richest appropriation of grace. Wesley writes, "Christ liveth in me— and therefore all that is holy, and just, and good."[62] Christian perfection, therefore, is love replacing sin, love conquering every vile passion and temper, love resplendent in the restored *imago dei*. Indeed, when the first Methodist Conference considered these same issues in 1744, it was agreed that no wrong temper contrary to love remains in the soul; all thoughts, words, and actions are governed by pure love.[63] There is nothing higher than this.

The Way to Christian Perfection

In his sermon *The Scripture Way of Salvation,* Wesley affirms that good works are in some sense necessary for full salvation. Earnest believers should employ all the means of grace at their disposal such as prayer, receiving the Lord's Supper, reading the Scriptures, and fasting.[64] Beyond this, they should engage in works of mercy such as "feeding the hungry, clothing the naked, entertaining the stranger, [and] visiting those that are in prison or sick. . . ."[65] "This is the way," Wesley admonishes, "wherein God hath appointed his children to wait for complete salvation."[66]

Though these works just enumerated are "good" strictly

speaking, since the sanctifying grace of God precedes them, and though they are in some sense necessary for Christian perfection, they are not necessary in the same sense as faith nor in the same degree. They are only conditionally required, if there be time and opportunity for them. But one cannot be saved to the uttermost without faith. Notice the subtle distinctions Wesley makes in the following:

> . . . for this repentance and these fruits are only remotely necessary, necessary in order to the continuance of his faith, as well as the increase of it; whereas faith is *immediately* and *directly* necessary to sanctification. It remains that faith is the only condition which is *immediately* and *proximately* necessary to sanctification.[67]

Faith alone, then, is both necessary and sufficient to establish the highest spiritual life in the heart of the believer. It is necessary in that entire sanctification cannot occur without it, no matter how numerous or selfless the works of mercy, and it is sufficient in the sense that even if only faith is present, one may be sanctified. Moreover, the marks or traits of this faith which establishes Christian perfection entail a divine evidence or conviction in three areas: first, that God has promised perfect love in the Scriptures; second, that what God has promised He is able to perform, and third that God is both able and willing to sanctify now.[68]

Interestingly enough, in contemporary Methodism, there has been a considerable degree of discussion—some of it heated—concerning the third aspect: namely, when entire sanctification occurs. Is it, on the one hand, to be received instantaneously in a crisis event or is it, on the other, to be received gradually as one matures spiritually? Wesley himself seems to emphasize different elements in various writings, and this is, no doubt, part of the problem. For example, in one place he argues that entire sanctification is "constantly both preceded and followed by a gradual work,"[69] with the implication that a good deal of time passes before this grace is received. But in his sermon *The Scripture Way of Salvation,* the instantaneous element appears virtually alone: "Look for it then every day, every hour, every moment,"[70] he urges.

Now these two statements just cited are not contradictory so long as it is realized that, for Wesley, the issue of process/instantaneous is a reflection of the larger issue of the relation between faith and works. Gradualism, therefore, highlights the normal spiritual development, the works, and the obedience that are conditionally required if sanctification is to occur. The instantaneous motif, on the other hand, keeps before the believer the unconditional element of faith—that perfection in love may yet occur even if only this ingredient is present. Wesley writes:

> And by this token may you surely know whether you seek it by faith or by works. If by works, you want something to be done first, before you are sanctified. You think, "I must first be or do thus or thus." Then you are seeking it by works unto this day. If you seek it by faith, you may expect it as you are: and if as you are, then expect it now.[71]

Yet another way of viewing this same problem is to consider it against the backdrop of Wesley's apparent distinction between ideal and practice. Thus, for instance, he writes in his *Brief Thoughts on Christian Perfection* that the reception of perfect love is generally just prior to death, "the moment before the soul leaves the body."[72] However, later in this same piece he notes, "I believe it may be ten, twenty, or forty years before."[73] And in the sermon *The Scripture Way of Salvation* he advises: "Certainly you may look for it *now*."[74]

What all of this means, then, is that Christian perfection is a present possibility for all who are born of God and believe. But, regrettably, only a few will have the quality of faith required until just prior to the crisis of death. That is, there is often a lengthy process of spiritual development which prepares one for the reception of this faith, even though, ideally, it can be received in a moment.[75] With these distinctions in mind, it nevertheless appears that Wesley emphasizes the immediate availability of this grace, especially in his Standard Sermons. He probably reasoned this way: If this faith can be received now— and it surely can be—then it must be preached now. And so he acted accordingly.

But suppose one is content with the grace of regeneration and does not, therefore, seek to be free from inbred sin or to progress spiritually. Can such a person prosper without pressing on? More important, can such a person continue to enjoy the grace already given? Since the basic trajectory of Wesley's theology is forward-looking, goal-directed, and teleological,[76] one would expect a negative answer to these ques-

tions. And this is precisely what is found. For the leader of the
Methodist revival, to fail to make progress, to refuse to repent
of the carnal nature, does not mean that one retains all of the
graces already received. Instead, one actually regresses. One
must, therefore, earnestly and sincerely seek to improve the
grace already given in order to remain spiritually healthy.
Christian perfection may yet be a way off, but not to go
forward, whether through fear or complacency, is in actuality
to go backward. There is no standing still.

NOTES

[1] Baker, *Works,* 25:12.
[2] Theodore W. Jennings, Jr., "The Myth of Aldersgate: The
Subversion of Wesleyan Theology," paper presented at the American
Academy of Religion, Boston, Mass., 5 December, 1987.
[3] Curnock, *Journal,* 1:478.
[4] Ibid., p. 482.
[5] Outler, *Works,* 2:226–27. (*Heaviness Through Manifold Temptations*) These disorders constitute what elsewhere Wesley refers to as
"infirmities." Cf. *A Plain Account of Christian Perfection,* Jackson,
Works, 11:396–97ff.
[6] Ibid., p. 227.
[7] Ibid., p. 231.
[8] Ibid., p. 229.
[9] Ibid., pp. 231–32.
[10] Ibid., p. 206. (*The Wilderness State*)
[11] Ibid.
[12] Ibid.
[13] Ibid., p. 220.
[14] Ibid., p. 234. (*Heaviness Through Manifold Temptations*)
[15] Ibid., 1:320. (*On Sin in Believers*)
[16] Ibid.
[17] Ibid. pp. 317, 321, and 323. Note that the Wesleyan quadrilateral *is* present in Wesley's theological writings after all. In fact, in his
two sermons *On Sin in Believers* and *The Repentance of Believers,* it is not
too much to say that the quadrilateral is prominently displayed.
[18] Ibid., p. 317.
[19] Ibid., p. 318.
[20] Ibid., p. 323.
[21] Ibid.
[22] Ibid.
[23] Ibid., p. 328. Wesley's harmartiology here has often been
misunderstood. The reference to Luther's idea of *simul justus et peccator*
in this context, found in both Outler (*Works,* 1:323 n.42) and Williams

(*John Wesley's Theology Today*, p. 129) is inappropriate. For Luther, this expression also means that the believer is not free from actual, outward sins, a teaching that Wesley clearly repudiates in this sermon. In his *Lectures on Romans,* the German Reformer writes, "Note that one and the same man at the same time serves the law of God and the law of sin, at the same time is righteous and sins!" Cf. Hilton C. Oswald, ed., *Luther's Works,* vol. 25, *Lectures on Romans* (Saint Louis: Concordia Publishing House, 1972), pp. 336ff.

24On two occasions when I served as a guest preacher and delivered a message of freedom from the guilt and the power of sin as the prerogative of the children of God, I was opposed by the pastor. In the first instance, which was in Brooklyn, the pastor said that people have come all the way from New Jersey to attend service, and how dare I preach such a message. Actually, at this point I was simply reading verbatim from the First Letter of John, an epistle to which the pastor obviously took great offense. The second instance concerned a Methodist minister who insisted on making a lengthy editorial comment after my sermon to the effect that we are all sinners, and we sin by thought, word, and deed every day. But is this Methodist theology?

25Ibid., p. 141. (*Satan's Devices*)

26Ibid. See Outler's note number 24 in which he points out that this material corresponds to significant events in the life of Wesley himself, especially after his Aldersgate experience when he lacked joy and walked in heaviness of spirit.

27Ibid.

28Ibid.

29Ibid., p. 142.

30Ibid., p. 144.

31Ibid., p. 146.

32Ibid. This makes clear the grave danger, regardless of the motive, of referring to regeneration as "mere" regeneration.

33Ibid., p. 147.

34Ibid., p. 149.

35Ibid.

36Outler, *Works,* 1:336. (*The Repentance of Believers*)

37Wesley, *NT Notes,* p. 15 (Matt. 3:8).

38Outler, *Works,* 1:335. (*The Repentance of Believers*)

39Ibid., p. 336.

40Ibid., pp. 344–45.

41Ibid., p. 345.

42Ibid.

43Ibid., p. 346.

44Ibid. Note that the language of "secondness" is very much a part of Wesley's vocabulary, as the sermon *The Repentance of Believers* clearly shows. Such language did not originate in nineteenth-century Methodism.

45 Ibid., p. 402. (*The Circumcision of the Heart*)

46 Ibid., p. 403.

47 Ibid., 2:101. (*Christian Perfection*)

48 Ibid., p. 102.

49 Ibid., p. 103.

50 Ibid., p. 104. Cf. Wesley's sermon *Heaviness Through Manifold Temptations,* Outler, *Works,* 2:202–21.

51 Ibid., p. 98.

52 Ibid., pp. 104–05.

53 See Outler's note 57, Vol. 2:105., where he indicates that Wesley's designation of fathers as those who are properly called Christians is much too strong, and it was later revised in 1750 to read, "these only are *perfect* Christians." (Emphasis mine)

54 Ibid., p. 105. This leads to a problem with Outler's interpretation as displayed in his introductory material to this sermon where he states that Christian perfection in its fullness leads to "the recovery of our negative power not to sin. . . ." However, such is the prerogative, as Wesley clearly indicates, even of babes in Christ. Perhaps Outler has confused the aspects of act and state in Wesley's doctrine of sin. Cf. Outler, *Works,* 2:97.

55 Ibid., p. 106.

56 Ibid., p. 117.

57 Ibid., p. 127. (*Wandering Thoughts*)

58 Ibid., p. 132.

59 Ibid., p. 133. Wandering thoughts in this sense may be understood as yet another instance of an infirmity, from which no one can be free. Cf. *Christian Perfection* 2:103ff.

60 Ibid., p. 119. (*Christian Perfection*)

61 Ibid.

62 Ibid., p. 118. See also Wesley's sermon *On Perfection* where he utilizes Paul's argument in Philippians chapter two to show that Christ is the model, standard, and guide of the Christian life at its greatest heights. Outler, *Works,* 3:74.

63 Jackson, *Works,* 11:387.

64 Outler, *Works,* 2:166. (*The Scripture Way of Salvation*)

65 Ibid.

66 Ibid.

67 Ibid., p. 167. These distinctions between conditionally-unconditionally, remote-directly are similar to the ones that Wesley made in terms of the approach to the new birth, but with one important difference: the former works are good, but the latter are not. This difference can also be understood in terms of the distinction between prevenient and sanctifying grace.

68 Ibid.

⁶⁹Jackson, *Works,* 11:442.

⁷⁰Outler, *Works,* 2:169. (*The Scripture Way of Salvation*)

⁷¹Ibid.

⁷²Jackson, *Works,* 11:446.

⁷³Ibid. Also note that Wesley again makes a distinction between ideal and practice as recorded in the Conference Minutes of 1744 where it reads, "Is this ordinarily given till a little before death? It is not, to those who expect it no sooner. But may we expect it sooner? Why not? For, although we grant, (1) That the generality of believers, whom we have hitherto known, were not so sanctified till near death . . . yet all this does not prove, that we may not be so today." Cf. *A Plain Account of Christian Perfection* in Jackson, *Works,* 11:387.

⁷⁴Outler, *Works,* 2:169. (*The Scripture Way of Salvation*)

⁷⁵This emphasis of Wesley's was somewhat modified in the Holiness revival of the nineteenth century, especially through the "altar theology" of Phoebe Palmer which tended to equate dedication with entire sanctification so that if the "gift is on the altar, the altar sanctifies the gift." This view tilts the delicate balance between divine initiative and human response and moves in the direction of humanity ability. But for Wesley, it is not dedication which sanctifies but faith. Moreover, Wesley understood the origin and development of this faith basically in terms of a sacramental context, in the utilization of the means of grace. For an extensive and more favorable treatment of the life and work of Phoebe Palmer cf. Charles Edward White, *The Beauty of Holiness: Phoebe Palmer as Theologian, Revivalist, Feminist, and Humanitarian* (Grand Rapids: Zondervan/Francis Asbury Press, 1986).

⁷⁶Clarence Luther Bence, "John Wesley's Teleological Hermeneutic" (Ph.D. dissertation, Emory University, 1981), p. 1.

Conclusion

ON READING WESLEY'S SERMONS:
The Structure of the Fifty-Three Standard Sermons

ARE THE STANDARD SERMONS ARRANGED IN A DEFINITE ORDER?

Wesley published four volumes of sermons in the years 1746, 1748, 1750, and 1760 respectively. These sermons, forty-three in all, though soon to become forty-four by the inclusion of *Wandering Thoughts* in 1762, received authoritative sanction through his subsequent action of preparing a Model Deed in 1763, which served as a guide for those preachers under his care. In 1771, he added ten other sermons, *Wandering Thoughts* among them, to the original forty-three, bringing the total to fifty-three. It should be immediately added, however, that sixteen years later, in 1787—probably out of a concern for a technical and legal matter relating to the Model Deed—he again reverted to the forty-four. Nevertheless, since nearly every contemporary American edition of Wesley's Standard Sermons, unlike the British,[1] includes the nine additional sermons, it is the structure of the fifty-three which will be considered here. This inclusion makes sense not only on practical grounds in terms of what sermons the faithful are, in fact, reading, but also because numbered among them are such important pieces as *On Sin in Believers, The Repentance of Believers,* and *The Scripture Way of Salvation.*

As this present study has clearly shown, the Fifty-Three Standard Sermons are remarkable in that they contain so little theoretical or speculative discussion. They are, instead, discourses on practical divinity and treat the two significant questions Wesley continually held before his congregations:

one, how do I become a Christian, and, two, how do I remain one? This emphasis is amply described by Outler who asserts that the Standard Sermons "contain the gist of [Wesley's] understanding of the essentials of religion."[2] Moreover, Sugden observes that in these homilies, Wesley is not concerned "with the whole round of Christian orthodoxy, [but with] the doctrines of sin and salvation."[3]

Though the theme of these sermons is apparent, the structure is less so, despite protests to the contrary. To be sure, Wesley himself wrote that he wanted to arrange them "under [their] proper heads, placing those together which were on similar subjects and in such order that one might illustrate another."[4] But why, then, does the sermon *The New Birth* follow *Christian Perfection*? And why does *Original Sin* come after the discourses *Upon Our Lord's Sermon on the Mount*? Burwash, for his part, maintains that the Fifty-Three Sermons form "a complete and progressive view of the whole subject of experimental and practical divinity."[5] But again it is difficult, if not impossible, to determine just what this progression is. And although Outler describes the structure of the sermons in terms of three major divisions: variations on soteriology, the order of salvation, and the graciousness and fullness of grace,[6] this division is likewise not without its problems. In fact, this noted Wesley scholar later writes that "even a casual analysis of these 'first four volumes of sermons' [1771 edition] reveals that questions of chronology and provenance are incidental."[7] He, therefore, concludes, "Their order is shaped by the inner logic of Wesley's special view of the mystery of salvation."[8]

In light of these considerations, it is argued that the structure of the Standard Sermons is not to be found in their specific sequence, for all such designations along these lines appear to be artificial and forced, even if they are somewhat descriptive. The sermons, quite simply, are not arranged in a clear and definite order. And if it is claimed that they are, in fact, shaped by Wesley's inner logic, it is a logic which escapes the common reader. This is not to maintain, however, that the Standard Sermons do not evidence any order at all, for they clearly do. Though the sermons are not sequentially arranged, they nevertheless highlight an order which is typical of Wesley's best thought on the process of salvation. Just what is this order? It is none other than the Wesleyan *ordo salutis*.

THE STRUCTURE OF THE *ORDO SALUTIS* DISPLAYED IN THE SERMONS

Wesley's preference for a theology centered in an order of salvation can be discerned not only in his theological pieces and correspondence, but within the structure of some of his more important sermons as well. In *The Circumcision of the Heart,* for example, which was preached at Oxford University in 1733, there is a "processive structure; each of the four virtues of humility, faith, hope and love is a successive stage in a process of salvation."[9] On a more psychological and developmental level, the process of salvation is evidenced by a transition from the natural to the legal and finally to the evangelical state as presented in the sermon *The Spirit of Bondage and Adoption.*

However, the clearest expression of the process of salvation is found in the sermon *The Scripture Way of Salvation,* produced in 1765. In this piece, Wesley tracks the first glimmer of prevenient grace upon the darkened soul to the full restoration of the *imago dei* in the heart of the believer through the graces of entire sanctification. In a real sense, this sermon is the gateway to all the others, for it epitomizes the entire corpus and highlights the motif of practical divinity. This sermon should, therefore, be read *first.* In other words, whatever order does emerge in the Standard Sermons must be distilled from the entire collection under the guidance of this key sermon. Once this initial task is accomplished, the reader can then proceed to examine the remaining sermons, always keeping in mind the structure discovered earlier. Such an approach is valuable for it facilitates a more profitable reading of the Standard Sermons[10] by giving the reader a sense of orientation at the outset, which does not emerge from any sequential reading.

Moreover, while exploring the trajectory of redemption in *The Scripture Way of Salvation,* Wesley considers at each major step along the way the structural relationship between the two major doctrines of justification and entire sanctification in terms of the place for law, works, repentance, faith, and the witness of the Spirit. Indeed, so preoccupied was Wesley with this structured way of thinking about salvation that Lindström notes, "The same conception of salvation as an ascent by steps was [even] applied to the organization of the Methodist societies. They were organized in classes and bands; there were also select bands or societies."[11]

The framework, then, that eventually rises from the Standard Sermons through the use of *The Scripture Way of Salvation* as an interpretive device reveals both the goal orientation of Wesley's preached theology *and* the structural connection between justification and entire sanctification and their respective supporting doctrines. This order can perhaps best be portrayed by the image of a large modern suspension bridge whose purpose is to carry traffic in one direction only (goal orientation). Continuing this analogy, the two main columns which support the bridge and which mark off significant points on the journey can be referred to as justification and entire sanctification. And though the second column represents a closer approach to the ultimate goal than does the first, the chief structural relation between them is one of parallelism.

This last point can easily be illustrated by a number of examples drawn from Wesley's preached theology. First of all, in his sermon *The Original, Nature, Property, and Use of the Law,* Wesley describes three initial uses for the moral law: "To slay the sinner is, then, the first use of the law; to destroy the life and strength wherein he trusts. . . . The second use of it is, to bring him unto life, unto Christ that he may live. . . . The third use of the law is to keep us alive."[12]

These three functions of the law, which are chiefly descriptive of the process leading to justification and initial sanctification, are mirrored in the believer's approach toward Christian perfection. Indeed, Charles Wilson notes, "In its activity of keeping a believer alive in Christ, that is, in promoting sanctification in the believer, the law has three specific uses."[13] These three further functions as expressed by Wesley include the following:

> We have not done with this law: for it is still of unspeakable use, first, in convincing us of the sin that *yet remains* both in our hearts and lives . . . *secondly,* in deriving strength from our Head into His living members, whereby He empowered them to do what his law commands; and *thirdly,* in confirming our hope of whatsoever it commands and we have not yet attained.[14]

Although the similarities are striking, note the differences here as well; the first set of uses revolve around the issue of actual sin, the latter around inbred sin.

Second, concerning the notion of repentance and its place in his order of salvation, Wesley specifically taught that "there is a repentance consequent upon, as well as a repentance previous to justification."[15] Therefore, in his commentary on Matthew 3:8, for example, he remarks, "Repentance is of two sorts; that which is termed legal, and that which is styled evangelical repentance. The former . . . is a thorough conviction of sin. The latter is a change of heart (and consequently, of life) from all sin to all holiness."[16] Thus, Wesley affirms that the legal repentance brought about through the gracious activity of the Holy Spirit and the ministrations of the law is necessary "in order to our entering into the kingdom of God,"[17] while evangelical repentance is necessary "in order to our continuance and growth in grace."[18]

Now, of course, there are important differences between these two kinds of repentances; however, these differences do not undermine the basic parallelism already noted. In other words, on one level these two doctrines are similar. But on another level they are remarkably different due to the spiritual growth that has taken place between the first and second kinds of repentance. This blend of similarity and difference noted here and elsewhere is characteristic of Wesley's structured way of thinking about the processes of salvation; indeed, it is one of his major soteriological fingerprints.

Third, in exploring the issue of the necessity of works prior to justifying faith, Wesley draws an important distinction between condition and degree in his sermon *The Scripture Way of Salvation*. He asserts, "Therefore both repentance, and fruits meet for repentance are in some sense, necessary to justification. But they are not necessary in the same sense with faith, nor in the same degree; for those fruits are only necessary conditionally; if there be time and opportunity for them. Otherwise, a man may be justified without them."[19] When Wesley addresses this same issue, but this time in terms of works prior to entire sanctification, he employs almost *exactly the same language*. He continues:

> Repentance and its fruits are necessary to full salvation; yet they are not necessary either in the same sense with faith, or in the same degree:—Not in the same degree; for these fruits are only necessary *conditionally,* if there be time and opportunity for them; otherwise, a man may be sanctified without them.[20]

But this similarity of language, utilized to describe the necessity of works preceding both justification and Christian perfection, must not, once again, obscure the significant difference between these works, for Wesley clearly taught that, properly speaking, works previous to justifying faith are not good while those works which flow from such faith are. This means, of course, that the theological interpretation of Wesley's conception of the nature and function of works preceding entire sanctification, for instance, must take into account not only the parallel of how Wesley viewed works prior to justification, but must also include any distinctive elements of the doctrine under review due to its own specific positioning within the Wesleyan *ordo salutis*.

Fourth, in his sermon *Justification by Faith*, Wesley maintains that "Faith . . . is the necessary condition of justification; yea, and the only necessary condition thereof."[21] And elsewhere he remarks, "I have continually testified in private and in public that we are sanctified as well as justified by faith . . . *exactly* as we are justified by faith, so are we sanctified by faith. Faith is the condition, and the only condition of sanctification, *exactly* as it is of justification."[22]

In addition, Wesley defines both justifying and sanctifying faith in terms of a divine evidence or conviction. But here the similarity ends, for in justifying faith the divine evidence or conviction is "a sure trust and confidence that Christ died for my sins."[23] But in entirely sanctifying faith the divine evidence or conviction is described as follows: "First, that God hath promised it (entire sanctification) in the holy Scripture . . . secondly, that what God hath promised He is able to perform . . . thirdly, a divine evidence and conviction that He is able and willing to do it now."[24]

Wesley once more underscores this difference between justifying and sanctifying faith in his sermon *The Repentance of Believers*. In depicting that faith which is peculiar to the believer, he writes:

> But, supposing we do thus repent, then are we called to "believe the gospel."
>
> And this also is to be understood in a peculiar sense, *different from* that wherein we believed in order to justification . . . Believe . . . He is able to save you from all the sin that still remains in your heart.[25]

Fifth, the use of two levels of interpretation in terms of similarity and difference is likewise necessary for the description of the gradual/instantaneous tension with respect to the temporal elements involved in justification and Christian perfection. For example, Wesley claims that both justification and Christian perfection are instantaneous events which are preceded by a gradual work. However, the imagery he employs in each case is markedly different. Concerning justification, Wesley utilizes the imagery of birth with great effectiveness:

> A child is born of a woman in a moment, or at least in a very short time: afterward, he gradually and slowly grows, till he attains to the stature of a man. In like manner, a child is born of God in a short time, if not in a moment. But it is by slow degrees that he afterward grows up to the measure of the full stature of Christ. The same relation, therefore, which there is between our natural birth and outgrowth, there is also between our new birth and our sanctification.[26]

But with respect to entire sanctification, he appeals not to the imagery of birth, but to that of death:

> From the moment we are justified, there may be a gradual sanctification, a growing in grace, a daily advance in the knowledge and love of God. And if sin cease before death, there must, in the nature of the thing, be an instantaneous change; there must be a last moment wherein it does exist, and a first moment wherein it does not.[27]

Lastly, Wesley maintains that the two principal acts in the process of salvation, that is, justification and entire sanctification, are accompanied by both an indirect witness which operates largely through conscience and a direct witness which entails the Holy Spirit's witness to our own spirit. Concerning the latter and with respect to entire sanctification, he comments, "None therefore ought to believe that the work is done, till there is added the testimony of the Spirit, witnessing his entire sanctification, *as clearly as* his justification."[28]

Not surprisingly, and despite the parallel of the role of the Holy Spirit in justification and perfection, the content of each witness is distinct. To be sure, Wesley notes that "when we were justified, the Spirit bore witness with our spirit, that our sins were forgiven; so, when we were sanctified, he bore witness, that they were taken away."[29]

In light of these preceding six observations, it should be apparent by now that, on one level, Wesley employs *the same* vocabulary to describe the two quite different processes of salvation from the guilt and power of sin (justification and regeneration) on the one hand and the further work of salvation from the being of sin (entire sanctification) on the other. However, the mere observation of parallelism, with its emphasis upon similarity, is not an appropriate vehicle to convey the notion of movement, the dynamic flavor, implicit in Wesley's goal-oriented (teleological) theology. And this is precisely why it is also important to see the differences between these doctrines due to the soteriological distance (growth in grace) between them. Put another way, the similarity and differences of these doctrines, expressed in terms of parallelism and progression respectively, are at the heart of the basic order which the Standard Sermons evidence as the following diagram indicates:

	Justification	Entire Sanctification
The Law		
Similarity	Accusation	Accusation
Difference	Actual sin	Inbred sin
Repentance		
Similarity	Self-knowledge	Self-knowledge
Difference	Legal repentance	Evangelical repentance
Works Meet for Repentance		
Similarity	Conditionally necessary	Conditionally necessary
Difference	Not good (strictly speaking)	Good (Sanctifying grace)
Faith		
Similarity	Unconditionally necessary	Unconditionally (exactly as) necessary
Difference	A sure trust that "Christ died for my sins"	A sure trust that Christ is "able to save from all the sin which remains"
The Witness of the Spirit		
Similarity	Direct witness	Direct witness (clearly as)
Difference	Sins forgiven	Sin "taken away"

The implication for scholarship, therefore, of this dynamic nature of Wesley's theology is that it is not sufficient merely to explore his doctrinal statements or sermons within the context of their historical settings. Although this preliminary task is vital, one must think systematically as well, and determine the theological setting within the *ordo salutis* where each doctrine is found. In other words, once a specific doctrine is located within the Wesleyan order of salvation, it must be expounded with reference to what both precedes and follows it within that theological framework. This approach makes for a more intelligible reading of the Standard Sermons and reveals that although Wesley was not a systematic theologian in the sense of a Thomas Aquinas or a John Calvin, he was nevertheless highly consistent in his thinking about the process of salvation.

NOTES

[1] The British editions contain only the original forty-four (forty-three plus *Wandering Thoughts*) which were established by Wesley in the 1787–1788 edition of his published works. The British Conference in 1914 considered this edition authoritative, largely as a result of historical considerations. Nevertheless, Edward Sugden's edition of *The Standard Sermons of John Wesley* includes the nine additional sermons. However, they are set apart from the others, indicating the British Conference's judgment in the matter. Cf. Edward H. Sugden, ed., *Wesley's Standard Sermons*, 2 vols. (London: Epworth, 1921), 2:331ff.

[2] Outler, *Wesley's Works*, 1:44. (Bracketed material mine.)

[3] Sugden, *Standard Sermons*, 1:14. (Bracketed material mine.)

[4] Ibid., p. 14.

[5] Rev. N. Burwash, ed., *Wesley's Doctrinal Standards* (Salem, Ohio: Convention Book Store, 1967), p. iv.

[6] Outler, *Works of Wesley*, 1:45. See also Steve Harper's article, "Wesley's Sermons as Spiritual Formation Documents," in *Methodist History* 26 (April 1988): 133., where he puts forth the following schema: sermons 1–16: the essence of salvation, 17–40: the order of salvation, 41–53: the application of salvation. This designation, although not without its merits, appears to be forced as well, especially when it is observed that *Original Sin* (sermon 44) and *The Wilderness State* (sermon 46) are placed under "the application of salvation."

[7] Ibid.

[8] Ibid.

[9] Clarence L. Bence, "Processive Eschatology: A Wesleyan Alternative." *Wesleyan Theological Journal* 14 (Spring 1979):54.

[10] For example, as one reads the sermons *Salvation by Faith* or *The Repentance of Believers,* it should be continually noted where these sermons would fit in the order established in *The Scripture Way of Salvation.* When this is done, it becomes clear that the essential framework of the fifty-three is none other than the Wesleyan *ordo salutis* itself. For a complete and more technical discussion of these ideas, see Kenneth J. Collins, "A Hermeneutical Model for the Wesleyan *Ordo Salutis." Wesleyan Theological Journal* Vol. 19 No. 2 (Fall 1984): 23–37.

[11] Harold Lindström, *Wesley and Sanctification* (Wilmore, Ky.: Francis Asbury Publishing Co.), p. 122. (Bracketed material mine.)

[12] Outler, *Wesley's Works,* 2:15–16. (*The Original, Nature, Property, and Use of the Law*)

[13] Charles Randall Wilson, "The Correlation of Love and Law in the Theology of John Wesley" (Ph.D. dissertation, Vanderbilt University, 1959), p. 92.

[14] Outler, *Wesley's Works,* 2:17. (*The Original, Nature, Property, and Use of the Law*)

[15] Ibid., 2:164. (*The Scripture Way of Salvation*)

[16] John Wesley, *Explanatory Notes Upon the New Testament* (San Francisco: E Thomas Press; reprint ed., Salem, Ohio: Schmul Publishers, 1976), p. 15.

[17] Outler, *Wesley's Works,* 1:336. (*The Repentance of Believers*)

[18] Ibid.

[19] Ibid., 2:162-63. (*The Scripture Way of Salvation*)

[20] Ibid., 2:167.

[21] Ibid., 1:196. (*Justification by Faith*)

[22] Ibid., 2:163. (*The Scripture Way of Salvation.* (Emphasis mine.)

[23] Ibid., 1:194. (*Justification by Faith*)

[24] Ibid., 2:167-68. (*The Scripture Way of Salvation*)

[25] Ibid., 1:347. (*The Repentance of Believers.* (Emphasis mine.)

[26] Ibid., 2:198. (*The New Birth*)

[27] Thomas Jackson, ed., *The Works of John Wesley,* 14 vols. (Grand Rapids: Baker, 1978), 8:329.

[28] Ibid., 11:402. (Emphasis mine.)

[29] Ibid., p. 420.

BIBLIOGRAPHY

I. Primary Sources: Wesley

Baker, Frank, ed. *The Works of John Wesley,* 34 vols. New York: Oxford University Press, 1982.

Burwash, Rev. N. *Wesley's Doctrinal Standards.* Salem, Ohio: Convention Book Store, 1967.

Curnock, Nehemiah. *The Journal of the Rev. John Wesley, A.M.,* 8 vols. London: The Epworth Press, 1938.

Jackson, Thomas, ed. *The Works of John Wesley,* 14 vols. Grand Rapids: Baker Book House, 1978.

Outler, Albert C., ed. *The Works of John Wesley,* 34 vols. Nashville: Abingdon Press, 1984.

Sugden, Edward H., ed. *Wesley's Standard Sermons,* 2 vols. London: The Epworth Press, 1921.

Telford, John, ed. *The Letters of John Wesley, A.M.* 8 vols. London: The Epworth Press, 1931.

Wesley, John. *Explanatory Notes Upon the New Testament.* Salem, Ohio: Schmul Publishers, n.d.

————. *John Wesley's Sunday Service of the Methodists in North America.* Nashville: The United Methodist Publishing House, 1984.

II. Secondary Sources: Wesley

A. Books

Borgen, Ole E. *John Wesley on the Sacraments.* Grand Rapids: Zondervan/Francis Asbury Press, 1972.

Burtner, Robert W., and Chiles, Robert E., eds. *John Wesley's Theology: A Collection From His Works.* Nashville: Abingdon Press, 1982.

Cannon, William Ragsdale. *The Theology of John Wesley.* Nashville: Abingdon-Cokesbury Press, 1946.

Cell, George Croft. *The Rediscovery of John Wesley.* New York: Henry Holt and Co., 1934.

Deschner, John. *Wesley's Christology.* Dallas: Southern Methodist University Press, 1960.

Green, V.H.H. *The Young Mr. Wesley.* New York: St. Martin's Press, 1961.

Lindström, Harald. *Wesley and Sanctification.* Wilmore, Ky.: Francis Asbury Publishing Co., n.d.

Outler, Albert C., ed. *John Wesley.* New York: Oxford University Press, 1964.

Piette, Maximin. *John Wesley in the Evolution of Protestantism.* London: Sheed and Ward, 1938.

Rattenbury, J. Ernest. *The Conversion of the Wesleys*. London: The Epworth Press, 1938.

Rowe, Kenneth E., ed. *The Place of Wesley in the Christian Tradition*. Metuchen: NJ: The Scarecrow Press, 1976.

Schmidt, Martin. *John Wesley: A Theological Biography*, 3 vols. London: The Epworth Press, 1962.

Williams, Colin. *John Wesley's Theology Today*. Nashville: Abingdon Press, 1960.

B. Articles

Bence, Clarence L. "Processive Eschatology: A Wesleyan Alternative." *Wesleyan Theological Journal* 14 (Spring 1979): 54.

Burnett, Ivan Jr. "Methodist Origins: John Wesley and Alcohol." *Methodist History* 13 (July 1975): 3–17.

Collins, Kenneth J. "John Wesley and the Means of Grace." *The Drew Gateway* 56 (Spring 1986): 26–33.

_____. "A Hermeneutical Model for the Wesleyan *Ordo Salutis*." *Wesleyan Theological Journal*, Vol. 19, No. 2 (Fall 1984): 23–37.

_____. "John Wesley and Liberation Theology: A Closer Look." *The Asbury Theological Journal*, Vol. 42, No. 1 (Spring 1987): 85–90.

Hall, Thor. "The Christian's Life: Wesley's Alternative to Luther and Calvin." *The Duke Divinity School Bulletin*, 28 (May 1963): 111–26.

Harper, Steve. "Wesley's Sermons as Spiritual Formation Documents." *Methodist History*, 26 (April 1988): 131–38.

Holland, Bernard G. "The Conversions of John and Charles Wesley and Their Place in Methodist Tradition." *Proceedings of the Wesley Historical Society*, 38 (August 1971): 46–53.

Hynson, Leon O. "Christian Love: The Key to Wesley's Ethics." *Methodist History* 14 (October 1975): 44–55.

_____. "Creation and Grace in Wesley's Ethics." *The Drew Gateway*, 46 (1975–76): 41–55.

Jennings, Theodore W. Jr. "The Myth of Aldersgate: The Subversion of Wesleyan Theology." A paper presented at the American Academy of Religion, Boston, Mass., 5 December, 1987.

Outler, Albert C. "Beyond Pietism: Aldersgate in Context." *Motive*, Vol. 23, No. 8 (May 1963): 12–16.

_____. "John Wesley: Folk Theologian." *Theology Today*, 34 (July 1974): 63–82.

_____. "John Wesley as Theologian—Then and Now." *Methodist History*, 12 (July 1974): 63–82.

_____. "The Place of Wesley in the Christian Tradition." In *The Place of Wesley in the Christian Tradition*, pp. 11–38. Edited by Kenneth E. Rowe. Metuchen, NJ: The Scarecrow Press, 1976.

_____. "Towards a Re-Appraisal of John Wesley as a Theologian." *The Perkins School of Theology Journal*, 14 (Winter 1961): 8–9.

Smith, Harmon L. "Wesley's Doctrine of Justification: Beginning and Process." *The Duke Divinity School Bulletin*, 28 (May 1963): 88–98.

Watson, Philip. "Wesley and Luther on Christian Perfection." *The Ecumenical Review*, 15 (April 1963): 291–302.

III. Methodism

A. Books

Bassett, Paul M., and Greathouse, William M. *Exploring Christian Holiness: Volume 2 The Historical Development.* Kansas City, Mo.: Beacon Hill Press, 1985.

Bonino, Jose Miguez. *Doing Theology in a Revolutionary Situation.* Philadelphia: Fortress Press, 1975.

Chiles, Robert E. *Theological Transition in American Methodism: 1790–1935.* Nashville: Abingdon Press, 1965.

Oden, Thomas C. *Doctrinal Standards in the Wesleyan Tradition.* Grand Rapids: Zondervan/Francis Asbury Press, 1988.

Outler, Albert C. *Theology in the Wesleyan Spirit.* Nashville: Discipleship Resources, 1975.

Runyon, Theodore., ed. *Sanctification and Liberation.* Nashville: Abingdon Press, 1981.

Towlson, Clifford W. *Moravian and Methodist.* London: The Epworth Press, 1957.

B. Articles

Heitzenrater, Richard P. "At Full Liberty: Doctrinal Standards in Early American Methodism." *Quarterly Review*, Vol. 5, No. 3 (Fall 1985): 6–27.

Oden, Thomas C. "Methodist Doctrinal Standards: Reply to Richard Heitzenrater." *Quarterly Review*, Vol. 7, No. 1 (Spring 1987): 41–42.

IV. Miscellaneous

Jowett, M. A. *The Dialogues of Plato*, 2 vols. New York: Random House, 1937.

McNeill, John T. *Calvin: Institutes of the Christian Religion*, 2 vols. Philadelphia: The Westminster Press, 1960.

Morris, Leon. *The Apostolic Preaching of the Cross.* Grand Rapids: Eerdmans Publishing Co., 1955.

Oswald, Hilton C., ed. *Luther's Works.* Vol. 25, *Lectures on Romans.* St. Louis: Concordia Publishing House, 1972.

Pelikan, Jaroslav, ed. *Luther's Works.* 55 vols., Vol. 26: *Lectures on Galatians, 1535.* St. Louis: Concordia Publishing House, 1963.

Rupp, Gordon E., and Watson, Philip S., eds. *Luther and Erasmus: Free Will and Salvation*. Philadelphia: The Westminster Press, 1969.

Schaff, Philip, ed. *The Creeds of Christendom,* 3 vols. Grand Rapids: Baker Book House, 1983.

————. *History of the Christian Church*. Grand Rapids: Wm. B. Eerdmans Publishing Company, 1910.